FASHION

Other titles in
this series include:

CARS
COMPUTERS
FITNESS
HEALTH CARE
MUSIC

FASHION

by Kathleen Beckett

Series developed by Peggy Schmidt

Peterson's

Princeton, New Jersey

A New Century Communications Book

Library of Congress Cataloging-in-Publication Data

Beckett, Kathleen.
    Fashion / by Kathleen Beckett.
       p.   cm. — (Careers without college)
    "A New Century Communications book."
    ISBN 1-56079-220-5 .
    1. Fashion—Vocational guidance.   2. High school graduates—
Employment.   I. Title.   II. Series.
    TT507.B414   1992
    687'.023'73—dc20   92-27985

Art direction: Linda Huber
Cover photo: Bryce Flynn Photography
Cover and interior design: Greg Wozney
Composition: Bookworks Plus
Printed in the United States of America
10 9 8 7

ABOUT THIS SERIES

Careers without College is designed to help those who don't have a four-year college degree (and don't plan on getting one any time soon) find a career that fits their interests, talents and personalities. It's for you if you're about to choose your career—or if you're planning to change careers and don't want to invest a lot of time or money in more education or training, at least not right at the start.

Some of the jobs featured do require an associate degree; others only require on-the-job training that may take a year, some months or only a few weeks. In today's real world, with its increasingly competitive job market, you may want to eventually consider getting a two- or maybe a four-year college degree in order to move up in the world.

Careers without College has up-to-date information that comes from extensive interviews with experts in each field. It's fresh, it's exciting and it's easy to read. Plus, each book gives you something unique: an insider look at the featured jobs through interviews with people who work in them now.

Peggy Schmidt

ACKNOWLEDGMENTS

Many thanks to the following people who helped provide the information and photographs that appear in this book.

Ivan Bart, New Faces Division, Wilhelmina Models, New York, New York

Neil Baxter, Editor, *Occupational Outlook Quarterly*, Bureau of Labor Statistics, Washington, D.C.

Mike Beaty, Elite Models, Dallas, Texas

Cathy Caligari, Public Relations, National Retail Federation, New York, New York

John Callanan, Designer, John Callanan Milliner, San Francisco, California

J.P. Correa, Public Relations, Geoffrey Beene, New York, New York

Beth Dempsey, Owner, Images & Details, Stamford, Connecticut

Michael DeSouza, Associate Professor, Interior Design Department, School of Visual Arts, and Owner, Michael DeSouza Designs, New York, New York

Angel Dormer, Assistant to Todd Oldham, New York, New York

Marie Essex, Associate Chair, The Parsons School of Design, New York, New York

Susan Fiorito, Ph.D., Professor, Department of Clothing, Textiles and Merchandising, Florida State University, Tallahassee, Florida

Jack Fraser, Vice President, National Retail Federation, New York, New York

Joel Garrick, Director of Public Information, The School of Visual Arts, New York, New York

Patrick Hennesey, Director of Public Information, The Fashion Institute of Technology, New York, New York

Kathy Hughes, Public Relations, Esprit de Corps, San Francisco, California

Susan Jones, Fashion Department, The Pratt Institute, Brooklyn, New York

Deete Kearns, Public Relations, Lauren Sara, New York, New York

Steve Landry, C' La Vie Models, Inc., Los Angeles, California

The Library of The Fashion Institute of Technology, New York, New York

Karyn Lyons, Public Relations, Ralph Lauren, New York, New York

Ann Magnin, President, Magnin-Bizer Public Relations, New York, New York

Cynthia Rowley, Designer, Cynthia Rowley, New York, New York

Lisa Schiek, Public Relations, Gucci, New York, New York

Jan Still-Lindeman, Divisional Vice President, DeVries Public Relations, New York, New York

David Vando, Owner, Models Mart, New York, New York

Thanks, too, to Linda Peterson, for her editing expertise.

WHAT'S IN THIS BOOK

WHY THESE FASHION CAREERS?

The world of fashion offers some of the most creative ways to make a living. A sense of style, ideas on how to put different looks together and new ways of thinking about clothes and accessories are highly valued because the fashion business is vibrant and ever changing.

In this book you will find five fashion careers discussed in detail:

❑ Fashion designer

❑ Model

❑ Sales representative

❑ Window display designer

❑ Retail salesperson

They were chosen not only because they are essential to the creation and sale of clothes and accessories, but also because how well you do your job matters more than any formal schooling. That's not to say you shouldn't consider going to a fashion or design school to pick up technical skills or information, but a certificate or degree is not necessary to break into the business.

Getting your foot in the door is not always easy, but once you do, you will be given a chance to prove yourself. Show your stuff. Test your ideas. And work hard to make them happen.

These five careers are essential parts of a cycle that repeats itself season after season. First, designers create clothing and accessories they want customers to buy. Models display the fashions on runways and in magazines for store buyers and customers to see and buy. Sales representatives try to convince store buyers that their clothing lines are the ones store customers will go for. Window display designers showcase the clothes in store windows to catch the fancy of customers and pull them inside. Then salespeople go to work helping customers select items that will create the right look or complement their wardrobe. While the sale is being clinched, the fashion designers are already hard at work coming up with more clothes for next season.

Working in the fashion business can be exciting, creative and glamorous. But many jobs require hard work and long hours. The pay for beginners can be low. If you are one of those people who is in love with the idea of making some aspect of fashion your work, and you have the vision to recognize that talent and a commitment to being the best can get you somewhere, you will no doubt find satisfaction and success in the fashion industry.

Before you begin reading about each of these careers, find out what top designer Todd Oldham has to say about careers in the fashion business, and read about the humble beginnings of three famous people: Ralph Lauren, Geoffrey Beene and Dawn Mello.

TODD OLDHAM

on Who's Cut Out for the Fashion Business

odd Oldham was given the Perry Ellis Award for Best Young Designer in 1991 by the Council of Fashion Designers of America. *The New York Times* proclaimed that he was one of the most promising young fashion designers in the country, and *Rolling Stone* put him on its hot list as Designer of the Year in 1992. Not bad for a 30-year-old who has no formal fashion training.

Oldham showed his first collection in 1990; his show has become one of the highlights of New York's fashion week. Celebrities and club kids, the fashion press and fashion groupies pack the event, gear up to hoot and holler as rap star Queen Latifah or drag queen Billy Beyond take their turns on the runway.

Beyond the hipness and the hoopla are the clothes. Oldham's honors are deserved: He has injected a breath of fresh air into the stuffy world of high fashion in this country. Potholders sewn on jackets serve as pockets; sequined horses modeled on paint-by-number pictures decorate dresses; suits are stitched of fabric that resembles mosaics. Rock musicians, including the B-52s and Deee-Lite, wear Todd Oldham originals when they tour.

Oldham's company, L-7, includes his Todd Oldham collection and a line of blouses, Times 7. Although Oldham designs and lives in New York, most of the production of his clothing is done in his hometown, Dallas. In an undistinguished concrete bunker just off the Stemmons Freeway, some of the world's most exciting new creations are sewn, inspected and bagged by a small army of workers.

Oldham remains close to his family. His mother is president of the company, his grandmother is head of quality control, his sister works in customer relations and his brother designs buttons. Even his dad tried his hand in the business for a year before going back to his first love, computers. And, oh yes, weaving their way under the pattern cutting table and around the clothing racks are Oldham's seven dogs.

We asked him to talk about how he got started and to advise our readers about careers without college in the fashion business.

My mother and grandmother taught me to sew when I was nine. There was no gender put on any activity. We grew up without a lot of money, so we were constantly at the crafts table.

My first job was working in alterations at the Ralph Lauren store in Dallas for about four months. I got the job when they handed me a $1,000 lace dress and said, "Shorten it." So I did, and I guess I did it right. I've never heard of anybody else starting out in design by working in alterations, but it's a very valuable skill to learn—basically you're fixing someone else's mistakes. That four-month stint taking apart somebody's well-made clothes and putting them back together over and over and over played the most important role in what I know today. It was like fashion boot camp.

I never worked for any designer. I just figured out the process myself, made the samples, took them to the stores and sold them. Then my mom and I sewed up the orders and delivered them to the stores. The first store was Neiman Marcus in Dallas and I was 19.

After taking my designs to the stores, it just sort of magnified. I would do special groups—private label stuff for The Limited, Barney's, Neiman's, Saks, Bergdorf's and Bloomingdale's.

It took about five years for me to get established. I used to listen to buyers' requests. It's a mistake to try to please everyone. You have to mean something to a special group of people. One of the hardest things about working in this business during my first few years was getting cooperation from manufacturers and fabric vendors. People really don't want to deal with startups. They just want to deal with known designers. They don't understand about working with someone along the way. I have an elephant's memory and remember everybody who was a pill to me on the way up; I don't work with them now.

In 1989 I got a call from Onward Kashiyama, a Japanese company that was looking for a new American designer to back, and I thought I might as well give it a go. It was my big chance to have my own label. I have one assistant, six sample makers and a half dozen salespeople in New York. Of course, there's the factory in Dallas.

One of the hardest things for me right now is the amount of time it takes me to do my work. I work 30-hour days. I never design during the day. We leave the office about 8 P.M. and then I go home and design at night. It seems like I'm always at work. It's like building a giant concrete tower on sand because even though I'm doing very well right now, I never lose sight of the fact that it's all just for the moment. I constantly have to reinvent myself every few months and come up with a new product. Luckily fashion recycles itself quickly, so there's always another chance if you do happen to falter.

I love the process of design, securing fabrics and taking

an idea and watching it become a product. There are other rewards, too. Now that my name means something on charity events, I'm able to help raise money for some organizations that would probably be overlooked, like the American Suicide Foundation. I enjoy raising some bucks that can help people who have nothing to do with fashion.

Fashion is a good business for determined people who believe in themselves. It's a trying business, too, and pretty much of an obstacle course. It's one of the few industries you can participate in on many different levels. For example, most of my sales staff started out as receptionists or as salespeople in department stores.

There are a lot of jobs for people who have no paper credentials—look at me. I get a million resumes, which never mean anything to me because this industry is all about intuition and style. You have to have that special spark to succeed, at least the way we hire. We look for people who have personal style and lovely manners, people who are secure and grounded, because there are a lot of barracudas in this business. You have to have a thick skin to pick up the phone and call, call, call and hold your own even if people aren't nice or receptive.

I never went to fashion school; I just went to high school. I guess technical schools are probably good. But you can't teach creativity. I learned the necessary technical skills by practice, by playing around and playing around. To this day I make all the patterns. As a kid, I cut stuff out freehand. It's fine to go to a fashion school and get the technical information down. But don't pay attention to people who try to teach you how to be creative. Just believe in your own vision.

FAMOUS BEGINNINGS

Ralph Lauren, Chairman and Chief Executive Officer of Polo Ralph Lauren Corporation

Ralph Lauren worked part time during high school as a salesperson at Alexander's, a department store in Manhattan. His first job after school was an assistant buyer in the men's department at Allied Stores in New York.

Dawn Mello, Executive Vice President and Creative Director of Gucci Worldwide

Dawn Mello's first job was working at the former B. Altman & Co. in New York as the assistant to the fashion director.

Geoffrey Beene, President and Chief Executive Officer, Geoffrey Beene, Inc.

Geoffrey Beene's first job was working as a window display designer for I. Magnin in Los Angeles. The head of the store was so impressed with Beene's work that he encouraged him to try his hand at fashion design.

Regardless of whether fashion designers create scarves or one-of-a-kind T-shirts, elegant evening dresses or sneakers for children, they all have one thing in common: They love fashion. To make it in this field, you must live and die for fashion. The technical stuff can be learned. But the inspiration and dedication it takes to make a go of it in this highly competitive world is either in your blood—or it isn't.

When you think of a fashion designer, you probably think of the superstars, the celebrities with megabuck empires and jet-set lives. But most of the clothing you wear has been designed by someone you have never heard of and probably never will. Most of these "unknowns" work in a noisy factory or small office cubicle and never make in their lifetime what a superstar designer makes in a year. Still, they would not consider doing anything else for a living.

Designers fuel the fashion industry with their creations. Every piece of clothing, whether it's a skirt, shirt, swimsuit or sock, starts as a vision in a designer's head. Then it's sketched on paper and cut out in fabric, sewn and fitted and fussed with.

Designers typically produce four collections a year—fall/winter, spring/summer, resort and holiday lines. Their work provides jobs for everyone in the business, from seamstresses to store presidents, models to merchandisers.

If you are an avid reader of fashion magazines or like to spend your free time sewing your own clothes, give it a go. Some aspiring designers attend design school to pick up the necessary technical skills; others teach themselves. Whichever route you choose, you will need to prepare a portfolio of your ideas to get your first design job.

You will probably start out as an assistant, helping a designer find the right button for a blouse and making sure his or her coffee cup is filled. If you can show that you are capable and a constant source of good ideas, you can move up to the job of designer. If you come up with exceptional designs and get the right breaks, maybe, just maybe, you can become a household name, right up there with Donna and Calvin and Oscar and Ralph.

What You Need to Know

- ❑ Fabric (characteristics of materials; which are best for pleating, cutting on bias, etc.)
- ❑ Color (what colors work with each other)
- ❑ Costing of materials and labor
- ❑ Basic art history (for examples of and inspiration for clothing designs)
- ❑ Technical understanding of knits (hand and machine) a plus
- ❑ Basic anatomy (the body underneath the clothes)

Necessary Skills

- ❑ Sewing
- ❑ Pattern drafting (drawing pattern on paper)
- ❑ Draping (developing concept by placing fabric on model)
- ❑ Muslin making (cutting pattern from inexpensive fabric to test pattern)
- ❑ Sketching (putting ideas on paper)

Do You Have What It Takes?

- ❑ A flair for fashion (as demonstrated in your personal wardrobe choices)
- ❑ Ability to see a design in your head and put it on paper
- ❑ Determination to see a project through
- ❑ Personality to deal with difficult people

Education

Formal training is not essential to get into or be successful in fashion design. Still, 75 percent of the leading fashion designers on Seventh Avenue attended a design school. Coursework, a certificate or an associate degree in fashion design is recommended by many.

Licenses Required

None

Interview Essentials

A portfolio is a must. It should contain a resumé, which describes your fashion experience—whether it's a summer job working in a retail store or projects you worked on in fashion design courses. Include a number of design sketches. These are high-quality drawings that show in detail your ideas for a variety of garments—sportswear, coats, suits and evening wear. Attach swatches of fabrics you'd like to use with each one.

You should also prepare a "flat" of each piece of clothing. A flat is a kind of production blueprint in which you lay everything out, front and back. Flats are the kind of illustrations that would be sent to clothing producers to work from, so detail and clarity are important. Finally, it's a good idea to include sketches and flats of designs geared to the particular company, store or individual you hope to land a job with.

Job Outlook

Competition for jobs: very competitive

The recession of the early nineties left its scars—many retail stores closed, cutting down the number of markets for a fashion designer's labors. But experts say there is always a place for a talented achiever. Certain areas, such as children's wear and lingerie design, offer more opportunities than sportswear.

The Ground Floor

Entry-level job: assistant designer

Depending on the size of the organization, there may be one or many assistant designers who act as the designer's right hand and are involved in every aspect of fashion creation.

Beginners

- ❏ Shop for trim (locate buttons, braid, ribbon and other trim from wholesale sources)
- ❏ Sketch (put the ideas of the designer on paper)
- ❏ Research ideas (visit museums and libraries for inspiration and to gather information)

Experienced Designers

- ❏ Develop fashion concepts
- ❏ Supervise work of assistants, sewers, sample makers and pattern cutters
- ❏ Shop for fabrics (at showrooms, mills and fabric fairs in the U.S. and Europe)
- ❏ Oversee production of clothing line in U.S. and increasingly in factories in the Far East—Hong Kong, Taiwan and Korea
- ❏ Organize shows of collections (decide which outfits and accessories to present)

On-the-Job Responsibilities

Designers and their staff work nine to five and beyond. They put in as many hours, including evenings and weekends, as is necessary to produce collections four times a year. Overtime is the norm before each collection debuts.

Those who work for employers have little control over the hours they work and usually do not have the option of working part time. Freelance work, however, is available.

When You'll Work

No one gets a break until after a collection is complete. Since most people work for small employers, they may not get as many paid sick days, vacation days and holidays as do employees of bigger companies—it depends on the generosity of the employer.

Time Off

- ❏ Merchandise discounts (wholesale prices on clothing or fabric from design houses)
- ❏ Free admission to fashion shows, fundraisers and parties

Perks

Who's Hiring

- ❏ Major designers
- ❏ Manufacturers
- ❏ Pattern companies
- ❏ Major department stores with private labels (their own exclusive designs)
- ❏ Small boutiques
- ❏ Private customers

Places You'll Go

Beginners: occasional travel
Experienced designers: regular travel

Most designers travel several times during the year to France, Italy and Switzerland to buy fabrics and to Hong Kong, Taiwan or Korea to oversee clothing production.

Surroundings

Despite the glamour of the profession, most designers, except for the most famous ones, work in a small space in a factory amid the noise and bustle of pattern cutters and sample sewers. The upscale furnishings and windows that are standard in some offices are a luxury for fashion designers.

Dollars and Cents

The starting salaries of entry-level designers can be as low as $18,000, but most are in the $20,000s. Most experienced designers average between $30,000 and $50,000 a year. After five years in the field, however, a talented and lucky designer could be making a six-figure salary. Well-known designers are frequently given shares in the ownership of the companies they work for.

Designers who want to start their own lines should have enough personal savings to purchase fabrics and labor to create a dozen samples to take to stores for orders. You would also need to finance the production of orders for at least three months, the minimum amount of time it takes for stores to pay their bills.

Moving Up

No education, training or licensing is needed to move up. Advancement is based on talent—the ability to create successful, saleable or influential designs. Moving up often means changing employers every few years. Starting your own company usually involves seeking financial backing from an investor with deep pockets.

◆ **Where the Jobs Are**

There are more than 21,000 firms involved in various aspects of fashion manufacturing in all 50 states. Most are small, employing 50 workers or less. Although New York City has the most design firms, retail stores and manufacturers, other major regional markets are Chicago, Dallas and Los Angeles.

Several cities specialize in one area of fashion: Denver is a center for skiwear; Boston for bridal wear and coats; Miami for children's wear and swimwear; Philadelphia for outerwear and sportswear.

◆ **The Male/Female Equation**

Women outnumber men in fashion schools, but men are well represented as fashion designers. More than 80 percent of all workers in the apparel industry are women, but many of them are employed in the low-paying manufacturing positions.

◆ **Making Your Decision: What to Consider**

The Bad News

- ❑ The fashion business is fickle and goes through up and down cycles
- ❑ Possibility of having to work with difficult people
- ❑ Having to work in depressing surroundings
- ❑ Low starting salary
- ❑ Having to work long, hard hours

The Good News

- ❑ Creative work outlet for fans of fashion
- ❑ Opportunity to create work from start to finish
- ❑ Fun of being part of a glamour industry
- ❑ Potential to make lots of money
- ❑ Possibility of international travel

More Information Please

The following is a list of organizations for professionals in fashion design. You may want to write or call one or more to ask for information on design schools, internships, scholarships and contests.

The Council of Fashion Designers of America
1412 Broadway
New York, New York 10022
212-302-1821

The Fashion Group International
9 Rockefeller Plaza
New York, New York 10022
212-247-3940

Men's Fashion Association of America
240 Madison Avenue
New York, New York 10016
212-683-5665

International Association of Clothing Designers
240 Madison Avenue
New York, New York 10016
212-685-6602

American Apparel Manufacturers Association
2500 Wilson Boulevard
Arlington, Virginia 22201
703-524-1864

National Outerwear and Sportswear Association
240 Madison Avenue
New York, New York 10016
212-686-3440

Young Menswear Association
47 West 34th Street
New York, New York 10001
212-594-6422

Clothing Manufacturers Association of the USA
1290 Avenue of the Americas
New York, New York 10104
212-265-7000

WHAT IT'S REALLY LIKE

Kristine Lebow, 34,
swimwear designer for Jantzen, Inc.,
Portland, Oregon
Years in the business: seven

How did you break into the field?
I started on a freelance basis making patterns for various
companies in the Pacific Northwest. I worked for companies that manufactured sportswear, bodywear, leotards and
bridal wear and for pattern companies.

Was it a "usual" first job?
I wouldn't say pattern making is the preferred way to go.
Working as an assistant to a fashion designer is much
better.

What kind of preparation did you have?
I went to a two-year design school in Portland and got my
degree in apparel design when I was in my mid-twenties. I
was older than many of the students because I had gone to
college for a few years, then got married and had a family
before I decided to go back to school. But the school was
not recognized for its apparel design program, so starting
as a pattern maker seemed to be the easiest way to break
into the fashion industry.

What was the hardest aspect of working in this field during your first few years?

Keeping in mind not only what you want to do creatively and what you think looks good, but also keeping in mind the business side. In other words, will the design sell? Can the manufacturer make a profit? If we don't make money on it, there's no reason to do it. One of the hardest things has been realizing that if the sales force doesn't believe in a design, they're not going to sell it.

When did you break out of pattern making?

After one and a half years I got a job as an assistant for an evening wear designer in a small company. I did that for two years, but decided I wanted to make the switch to a bigger company—there really wasn't anywhere to move up to where I was. I got a job offer from Jantzen to work as a pattern maker. It was a step backward, but I felt it could be a good career move to go with a larger company. Shortly after I was hired, the designer of the swimwear line left, and I got promoted into the job.

What do you currently do?

I'm responsible for the initial concept—selecting the prints and the colors, the fabric, styling and fit. I go to New York several times a year to see fabric suppliers, most of whom have offices there. I design two collections a year; the first has 30 suits, the second has 70.

What do you like most about your work?

You get to create something out of nothing, taking all the possibilities and building something that's an identifiable product.

What do you like least about your work?

I really like my job but I guess I don't always get to do what I want. There are restrictions on what I can do. My boss, the merchandiser of the line, approves everything I do.

What was your proudest achievement?

When Princess Diana was photographed in one of my suits (a bright color-blocked bikini) and it made it into the national headlines.

What advice would you give to someone who was thinking of going into this field?

Develop your eye and look at everything you see. Look at designers and what they do. Isolate what makes a garment special or unique or interesting. Pay attention to how things fit. Even if you don't know why it does or doesn't, you can start to distinguish just by looking at what looks good and what doesn't. You will figure out why later.

Learn as much as you can about construction, color and fabrics. Draw all the time. Keep a notebook and sketch. Take illustrating classes—life drawing is really good because you will understand the body and how clothes fit on it. If you know what's underneath, you can draw a fashion sketch more easily.

Study a foreign language. Chinese, Japanese or Spanish are good choices because a lot of operations are moving to the Orient and Mexico for cheaper labor. If you can converse in the languages of those areas, you are an asset to a company.

Linus Mendenhall, 23,
design director of the
Susie Tompkins line of Esprit de Corps,
San Francisco, California
Years in the business: five

What do you do on your current job?

I lay out the plan for each season. I choose colors, fabrics, prints and yarn dyes, do the concept and pass it along to Susie for her approval. Then I work with my team of designers to get the product done.

What did you do before that?

I always knew I wanted to be a fashion designer. I've been sketching since age five. I came from a sports-oriented family and I was always dragged around to sports events. I'd sit in the bleachers with my paper and pen and resketch what everyone was wearing. When I was 12, I lied about my age and said I was 17 and worked with this natural cotton company. I met the owner and told her her designs weren't commercial enough! So she hired me. I started working with her, designing clothing from her fabric.

I saw my first Esprit catalogue in 1980 and thought it was fantastic. I loved their philosophy on fashion, so I set my mind on being a designer there. After high school I went to the Fashion Institute of Design and Merchandising in San Francisco. It was a two-year program but I became frustrated in my second year and left. I was dying to get out and *do* what I was feeling.

I was working at Macy's as a salesperson at the Esprit shop and one night Susie came in. I told her I wanted to work with her. I showed her my portfolio—it wasn't even a proper one, just concepts and rough sketches and fabric swatches, but I started working for her at her house, assisting her personally plus designing on the side for three years.

When Susie bought out Esprit from her ex-husband I started working for the company. If you want something bad enough and work hard enough for it, dreams will come true. So I started at Esprit in 1991 as an assistant designer. Within eight months I was made designer. A year after that I was made design director of Susie's line.

What kind of preparation did you have?
It was hands on. When I was a kid I ran home from school not to do my homework but to learn about pattern drafting and check out the magazines. That was my passion. When I got into fashion school, it only sharpened up the skills that I had taught myself. As a designer you don't do pattern drafting anymore—you have a pattern cutter.

What was the hardest aspect of the job during your first few years?
Trying to do something original and new, especially in the hard economic times we are in. It's such a conservative climate out there right now. And the logistics of fashion can be discouraging—sometimes there's a price point factor that determines the fabrics you can use.

What do you like most about your work?
I love the creativeness, the inspiration.

What do you like least?

It's hard work. It really is 98 percent sweat and 2 percent glamour. It's a numbers and paper job. There's only a small percentage of time when you get to sit down and be creative with sketching.

How long did it take you to get established?

That's still evolving. I'm still young. I have a lot to prove. As far as salary goes, I'm getting there, but I'm paying my dues.

What has your proudest achievement been?

I think my rapid growth and timing—I'm proud of that. And the work that I'm doing.

What advice would you give someone who is thinking of going into this field?

Really get to know a designer. Maybe do some intern work. See the business and find out if this is your true calling. It's not all runways and trips around the world. Get your foot in the door before you throw yourself into it. Get into fashion school and get a freelance job on the side. Hands-on training plus schooling never hurts. And don't give up on yourself—believe in your dream.

Brian Bubb, 35,
menswear designer and owner of
Bubb, a tie and men's shirt manufacturer,
New York, New York
Years in the business: 14

When did your interest in fashion begin?

Since I was a little boy growing up in York, Pennsylvania, I've been interested in sketching and drawing and fashion. I have pictures of myself at age five in ridiculous-looking checked suits with matching hats. I thought I was snappy. My family likes to joke about how I refused to lie down for a nap in kindergarten because I didn't want to wrinkle my suit, so the teacher stood me up in the corner.

My mom and dad were both fashion plates. And both grandmothers were very clever seamstresses. They had beautiful fabrics hidden away in their sewing rooms. I made gaudy shirts with big flowers and forties prints from them in high school. I visited New York and went to the stores, which further whetted my appetite. I thought, "I could go to school here and be part of this."

Did you?

After taking all the art courses I could in high school, I went to Parsons School of Design. I spent three years learning illustration and sketching and a bit of sewing. We had to make our own projects. The exposure to New York was phenomenal—its stores and the opportunity to meet designers at school.

What was your first job?

After graduating from Parsons in 1978, I got a job with Oscar de la Renta. He had a designer cattle call. He looked at everyone's book, and I guess he thought I was the one. But after a year I realized that I was not cut out to do the frou frou and the sequins that Oscar does so well, so I left. But while I was there, I was a design assistant—what we called a design "lackey." It was great because I got to do a little of everything. I learned where to get the best rhinestone buttons, where all the thread shops were and who had the best seam tape. I got to sketch and get involved in the sittings. I even learned how to put together licensing arrangements.

What was your next job?

I became the assistant to Bill Robinson when he was designing Calvin Klein Menswear. The pay was lower, but I thought it was something I'd like to try. I answered the phone and occasionally did sketches, but it wasn't very satisfying because Bill did everything.

After six months, I left to do freelancing. I worked for Ralph Lauren as a sketcher, did some designing for Kasper and sketched cartoon caricatures for HBO. Then I got an offer to help design for Marina Ferrari, Oleg Cassini's niece, who had her own women's line in Milan. She wasn't a designer in the classically trained sense, but I had a great time for a summer and met some wonderful people.

Did you stay in Europe?

After a trip back to New York, I returned to Europe. There

was an assistant's job in Paris with Christian Dior Monsieur, which I got. It had a lot more responsibility because the staff was small. Sketching was my number one responsibility. I did some fabric research and purchasing with my boss. I also worked with the American licensing programs and prepared all the information so the people back in the States knew what the season was going to look like.

Would you consider these first few years on-the-job training?
Definitely. Some people think they're going to become Calvin Kleins when they graduate. But the first five years on the job are still a learning experience. In Paris, I worked in the same room as the pattern maker, so I got to learn why a jacket was cut this way or why trousers were angled that way. I also hung out with the sewers. They were always thrilled to have one of the design assistants come up and talk to them because they're shoved up under the eaves. I also went to lunch with assistants who worked with other designers, something you could do in Paris because each designer had his or her own look and they're not insecure about the competition.

When did you come back to the United States?
Two years later. I got an offer to work with Perry Ellis on his new men's line with another assistant. In the beginning we had to learn the ropes and follow the rules because Perry had a very distinctive look. But then I was given the design of neckties as my own project. I worked with different silks—twill and matte. I learned how printing operates and how chemicals affect the coloring of the ink.

After a year the other assistant left and Perry said, "Darling, I'm not going to hire anyone else. You can be the big cheese. Just hire some assistants." I became director of design for Perry Ellis Menswear.

What kinds of things were you responsible for?
I dealt with all the problems and questions of the men's line. I reported to Perry and did what he wanted, but also gave him concepts and ideas about new colors and fabrics. My staff and I would have roundtable discussions of what to do for each season. We'd have muslins (samples) made and weekly fittings to make sure the garments were just right.

Was there a downside to working for a big company?
You have to answer to a lot of people when the stakes get
higher. Once Perry died, I just didn't enjoy it anymore
because everybody wanted to get their fingers in the pie.
They didn't understand what Perry did—that design is
where it all starts. It became more of a business run by
financial considerations. So after six years with Perry Ellis,
I left to start my own company, Bubb, to specialize in
men's neckties and shirts.

How did you launch it?
I used my entire savings to live on and to pay for the business, and I got a loan from a friend. It was tough. We
hooked up with a tiemaker who was going to purchase fabric for us and that fell through. That's typical. In the mean-
time, a friend of ours who worked in Japan said to send our
business plan to his boss who might be interested. He
wasn't. We sat around chewing our nails because we had to
show the line in two months and we had no showroom and
no money. Our break came when the Japanese company
changed its mind and did a licensing deal with us. That
company produces our ties and shirts exactly the same as I
do here.

Could you describe your business here?
We have a New York showroom, which buyers visit to see
our line. We sell to stores all over the country—Neiman
Marcus in Texas, I. Magnin in California and a lot of small
specialty stores. When you're selling wholesale, you have
to contact stores, develop a rapport and find out which ties
work for them. There are three of us in the showroom now.
We're thinking of taking on a sales agency and paying them
a commission because we can't get to the West Coast,
Texas and Florida, and they have sales reps all around the
country.

What else does running your own business involve?
You can no longer just design, you have to manage. There
are salaries and health benefits to pay. You have to ship the
merchandise, then send invoices and collect. The money is
supposed to come in 30 days, but when it doesn't, it can
disrupt your cash flow. You also have to figure out how
much the fabric and labor costs of producing different ties
are. For me, it's not nearly as much fun as designing.

When do you design?

At night when I get home. My inspirations often come in the middle of the night. The other night I had jet lag because I had just gotten back from Tokyo. About two in the morning, I thought, "I have to make a presentation!" So I started sketching away.

Are you going to expand your line?

I don't just want to be a tie designer. So I'm considering expanding into a whole lifestyle accessories collection— belts, small leather goods and suspenders. It's a natural progression.

What do you like most about what you do?

The biggest thrill for me is when someone says, "I bought one of your ties and shirts, which were a little wild, but every time I wear them, I get so many compliments." That says to me that I'm doing my job right. Seeing people on the street wearing the stuff is always great. I also like working with the press and the stylists.

What are the low points?

Thinking about money and making sure it's coming in is the biggest downer.

What advice would you give to someone who was thinking of going into this field?

If you go to the right design school and you're exposed to the best people, you'll learn a lot and make a lot of contacts. A lot of students get their first jobs because big-name designers critique their work while they're in school, and if they like it, they'll hire them afterward.

If you're near a big city, go to the museums there. You might see a beautiful brocade in a sixteenth-century painting and suddenly think, "I could do that in a jacket." A lot is self-education, keeping your eyes open and noticing which elements work well together.

If you enjoy being the center of attention and are a bit of an actor or actress, modeling may be for you since models must change "roles" from job to job. For every assignment you get, there's another lost because you weren't considered suitable, so it helps to remember that rejection also comes with the job. But if you have the right look, determination and lots of luck, rewards can be great.

You flip through the pages of the top fashion magazines and you see those stunning supermodels who make the clothes look gorgeous and the products appealing. Those who make it big earn a fortune, travel first class around the world and have the recognition, even adulation, of admirers. But such a life is for the lucky few. There's a lot more involved in modeling than appearing on the cover of *Vogue*.

21

Many models have enjoyable careers at the local level. They may work in area stores, appearing in fashion shows or doing informal modeling by walking around in various outfits the store wants its shoppers to see. Others work as fit models—the perfect size eight on which a designer actually pins and adjusts the sample of a new creation. Still others work behind the scenes in a designer's showroom, modeling clothes on a one-to-one basis for store buyers who want a closer look at the styles they've seen on the runway.

Even for models at the higher levels—those who've signed up with New York City agencies—there are various types of assignments. Appearing in advertisements pays the most. Editorial photography (pictures for magazine fashion spreads) pays far less but can be extremely prestigious. Runway shows are hectic but exciting. Catalog work pays the bills.

One critical factor in becoming a model is something you either have or you don't: youth. It's helpful for girls to start modeling part time while still in high school; males can be in their early twenties. Agencies like to have time to mold a model plus the guarantee of a long "run" on their investment. Modeling is, however, a short-lived career. Female models in their teens and twenties are in the biggest demand.

Besides being the right age, a hopeful model has to have the right stuff in physical terms. Having the required height and body measurements is essential, because a model must immediately fit into the clothes she will display—there's no time for alterations. In terms of photography, a model's bone structure is key. She must have a face that the camera loves, one that makeup and lighting can enhance even more. As for having the right "look," in recent years the blonde, natural, California-type model has been edged out by more exotic faces with stronger features. However, since tastes change quickly in this business, that preference may not last. Nobody knows what look will be the next in demand.

Within the world of modeling there are specialties. Body parts models have exquisite hands, legs, arms and other features. Large-size models can find photographic, fit and runway work, as can petite models.

What You Need to Do

The best way to launch a modeling career is to send a simple snapshot to the dozen or so top New York agencies and hold your breath. If they like what they see, they'll arrange for you to take a trip to New York for an interview. Though many hopeful models spend big bucks on professional photographs, the agencies say don't bother. And if they sign you on, that's when they'll put you in touch with photographers who will take pictures for a minimal fee, often just the cost of film and development (about $50 per roll).

Before those photos are taken, the agency will work with you on your hair, makeup and figure. After you have these "new and improved" pictures to show, the agency will start sending you on "go-see's" to magazines, photographers and other clients such as advertisers to get assignments.

Physical Requirements

❑ Required height (5 feet 9 inches to 6 feet 1 inch for females; 6 feet to 6 feet 2 inches for males)
❑ Required clothing size (dress size 6 to 8 for women; jacket size 40R for men)
❑ The right age when you break into the business (14 to 20 for females; early twenties for males)
❑ Good bone structure, with wide-set eyes, straight nose (full lips on females are currently a strong asset)

Do You Have What It Takes?

❑ Being responsible for showing up at assignments on time
❑ Ability to take direction (even if you question the good judgment of the client or photographer)
❑ Burning ambition
❑ A gracious winner/good loser attitude
❑ An upbeat, cheerful personality

❑ Patience (ability not to fidget or fuss during long fitting or photography sessions)
❑ Independence to live away from home at a young age
❑ Determination to keep your weight in check and your body in shape through healthy eating and exercise

Education

What about modeling schools? Most top New York agents maintain that an aspiring model can be equally successful if he or she contacts agencies directly. If the agency signs up a model, it will teach him or her what's needed.

Licenses Required

None

Job Outlook

Competition for jobs: highly competitive

Years ago, models specialized in working for certain types of employers: magazines, designers, catalogs or stores. There's less specialization today; the top models are in demand for *all* those kinds of modeling jobs, so a smaller number of models are getting the lion's share of the work. Although recessions can decrease advertising and editorial (magazine) budgets, the demand for models remains steady.

The Ground Floor

Entry-level job: model

Many new models who have just signed up with a New York agency are sent to Europe where work is more plentiful and magazines more willing to try new faces. This exposure can jump-start their careers and give them the necessary experience and pictures for their "book" (a portfolio that contains samples of their photo assignments). Another place for a beginner is as a showroom model, giving store buyers a close-up look at each design in the latest collection before they place their orders.

Beginners and Experienced Models

❑ Dress in clothes as directed
❑ Be patient as makeup and hair stylists continually adjust your appearance
❑ Follow instructions from photo stylists and photographers on how to look, move and perform

Work hours are unpredictable. A model may be signed up on a shoot of a few hours or a few days. On a location shoot the model is on call around the clock for the duration of the trip. How often you'll work depends on demand. Top models could work every hour of the day.

As is the case in any self-employed field, it is the model's decision when to schedule vacation time—without pay, of course.

❑ Invitations to "hot" clubs, restaurant openings and parties
❑ Discounts from designers

❑ Model agencies
❑ Stores (department stores and boutiques that stage fashion shows and don't hire models from agencies)
❑ Designers and design houses (for fitting and showroom models)

Beginners and experienced models: frequent travel
You'll be expected to pack your bag at a moment's notice for location shoots that might take place on balmy beaches or on an Arctic landscape.

They vary greatly. One day you might be modeling amid the ruins of ancient Greece; on another, you might be posing in a cramped, crowded studio shooting pictures for a catalog.

Dollars and Cents

The starting salary at most New York agencies is $150 an hour or $1,500 a day for catalog work. Star models can make as much as $12,000 a day for such work. Magazines have their own rate structures and may pay as little as a few hundred dollars a day, but the exposure is invaluable. Advertisers pay $3,500 a day to start; some top models have million-dollar-plus contracts with advertiser clients. Agencies make their money by taking a 15 to 20 percent cut of the fee paid to the model on any booking. The salaries of male models tend to be a little lower than those of female models.

Moving Up

Advancement is based on the ability to move or pose comfortably and expressively, having the right look at the right time, striking the fancy of an important photographer or magazine editor—and lots of luck.

Where the Jobs Are

A great deal of modeling work originates in New York. The top agencies are there; so are the editorial offices of leading fashion magazines, advertising agencies with national and international clients, and major fashion designers. Every major city, however, has agencies that place models in editorial assignments with local magazines, ad shoots for newspapers and television, and fashion shows. In addition, these local agencies are sometimes contacted by New York modeling agents who go on scouting trips across the country, looking for new faces. One piece of advice: beware of any agency that requires that you give them money before you can be one of its models. Reputable agencies make their money by charging clients a percentage of the fee being paid to a model for an assignment.

Schooling

There are reputable modeling schools whose programs include instruction on posture and walking; skin, hair and nail care; diet and exercise and wardrobe coordination. Be wary of schools that promise modeling jobs after graduation—it's a guarantee that's tough for any kind of school to make. Before you enroll in a school, check with your area Better Business Bureau to find out if complaints have been lodged by former students against the school.

The Bad News	*The Good News*
❏ Unsteady work	❏ Potential to make
❏ Lack of job security	lots of money
❏ Short-lived career	❏ Opportunity to travel
❏ Rejection	❏ Glamor
	❏ Recognition

◆ **Making Your Decision: What to Consider**

Female models far outnumber male models, although there is work for both.

◆ **The Male/Female Equation**

A good source of information is Models Mart, 42 West 38th Street, New York, New York 10018 (212-869-2020 or 1-800-223-1254). Owner David Vando and staff can answer questions about breaking into modeling and the reputation of schools and agencies around the country. They will also mail free guidelines and booklets on such topics as preparing a portfolio. The following directories, which are published by Peter Glenn, Ltd., are available in bookstores or by calling Models Mart. They include:

◆ **More Information Please**

The Madison Avenue Handbook (lists magazines, agencies, photographers)
The International Directory of Modeling and Talent (leading agencies and schools throughout the world)
The New York Modeling Agency Directory (various types of agencies, interviewing procedures)

WHAT IT'S REALLY LIKE

Helen Powers, 38,
fit model with Ford Modeling Agency,
New York, New York
Years in the business: 17

What does a fit model do?
I try on a garment and the designer or buyer takes a look.
After she makes her initial comments about the look, I usually talk about how the garment feels to me—if I have a
good rapport with her. I might say, "The angle of this
pocket makes me look a little heavy. If you move it over a
1/4 inch, it will be more slenderizing," or "The pockets are
a little too low." I have to be respectfully diplomatic. I
don't want to offend the pattern maker as he or she is the
artist who created the garment from a sketch.

How a garment moves is important, too. If I'm trying on a
straight skirt without a kick pleat or slit in the back, I
stretch my leg to see whether I could get on a bus. If I have
trouble pulling it up over my hips, I'll tell the designer—
after all, it's a pain if you can't do that when you go to the
ladies' room.

What are the requirements to be a fit model?
A perfect fit model is totally different from a runway or

photographic model. Measurements are everything—you must have certain shoulder and sleeve length, torso and inseam measurements. A few of the top fit models on Seventh Avenue are in their late fifties. Some fit models are beautiful, but the right measurements are most important.

I'm 5 feet 7½ inches. I fluctuate between 130 and 132 pounds. I'm a perfect size 8. My bust is 36 inches, my waist is 26½ inches to 27 inches (depending if it's before or after lunch), my high hip, which is 4 inches below the waist, is 34½ inches, and my low hip, which is 8 inches below the waist where the thigh and the derriere meet—the widest part of a woman—is 37½ inches.

How did you get started?
I started working part time in high school selling clothes, and I continued doing that while I went to a fashion school in Miami Beach. When I was 21, I went out to California and worked in sales in a designer's showroom. Somebody asked me what size I was, which happened to be a junior 9. It turned out that all my measurements were perfect for a fit model.

One thing led to another. I dressed nicely, which helps because designers want to have a model who looks fashionable. My background was in fashion, and I loved clothing and dressing nicely and being a professional career woman. Within a year or two, I had over 60 clients, and within four years, I was making $70,000 a year.

After about five or six years, I couldn't handle all the work, so I had other fit models work for me. When I couldn't take an assignment, I would send one of the models and charge her a 10 to 15 percent fee.

Was the work difficult in any way?
It was tough to be on your feet 12 hours a day, and I burned out. Then I gave it up for a few months. I had been living in Los Angeles for nine years and decided I needed the energy, momentum and excitement of New York, so I moved. But then it was like starting all over again with my career.

Didn't your years of experience help?

The people in New York didn't care who I had worked for in Los Angeles. And like a lot of California models, I was independent—I didn't work for an agency. But that's not the case in New York. Fortunately, I started getting accounts by calling up manufacturers I heard about. Chaus was one of my first accounts. I later signed with an agency and went from it to a more established one. And then my booker went to the Ford agency, and I followed.

What are salaries like for fit models?

They now get $150 to $175 an hour in New York, not including the 15 to 20 percent service fee which the agency charges the manufacturer. I work eight hours a day, year round. During slow times—Chinese New Year's when the factories in Hong Kong close for two weeks and the first two weeks of July when U.S. mills are closed—I might work a five-hour day. A very busy day could be 12 hours.

What do you like most?

I still find it exciting to try on new fashions. And every day is something new; every day I fit for different clients. I may work for the same clients a few times a week, but it's a different schedule every day, which keeps it fresh and exciting.

It can be very glamorous, too. I've traveled to Hong Kong when the schedule was tight. One time, a large retail company flew me overnight to Paris, then sent a Lear jet to pick me up in Paris and take me to Florence to try on jeans for a meeting with all the buyers in Europe.

What do you like least?

Watching my weight. And the unpleasant conditions in some factories. They're old. One time, when I was changing clothes in a bathroom, I spotted a mouse. On the other hand, the surroundings can be very glamorous.

What has your proudest achievement been?

Being good at what I do. Being appreciated makes me feel accomplished.

What does it take—beyond measurements—to make it as a fit model?

An extreme amount of patience. You can be in one garment

up to an hour discussing the detailing between collar spread, the sleeve length or buttons. I treat every garment the same, whether I'm fitting it for a less expensive manufacturer or the couture. After all, the $1,000 couture dress may be a one-of-a-kind, but they may be cutting 10,000 of that one style for a department store.

James Edwards, 31,
model with L.A. Models,
Los Angeles, California
Years in the business: eight

What are the requirements for being a male model?
You have to be at least 6 feet tall. I'm just under 6 feet 1 inch and have brown hair and hazel eyes. My jacket size is the standard 40 regular. I have a strong build, so I get jobs that require an athletic look. I've done editorial work for men's fitness magazines and ads for Speedo and Reebok. I'm lucky because I can keep my muscles toned up by just working out once a week.

How did you get started in modeling?
When I was in high school in Bad Axe, Michigan, I worked part time in a men's clothing store as a salesperson. I started modeling in their little fashion shows—tuxedos for bridal shows and things like that. While I was in college, I also worked in a top men's clothing store, Bigsby & Kruthers in Chicago. I got into fashion shows, photographers started taking pictures and I began getting my portfolio together.

In 1982, when I was 22, I moved to California. I was a little too old to model boys' clothing, but not quite old enough looking for men's, so I finished school and became a regional manager for some clothing shops from Milan. Then I decided to try to get back into modeling.

I didn't feel like I needed to go to modeling school, because I feel you either have it or you don't. I got some photography students from a local art college to take pictures for me.

An agency called Privilege took me on, got my first comp, or composition, which is a little array of pictures that it sent out to clients. I started going to castings and getting work. After that, I switched to an agency called L.A. Models; the division I now work for—L.A. Talent—takes some of your older dinosaurs like me.

What sort of assignments do you get?

There is a demand out here for two kinds of models. Beachwear clients want surfer types with blond hair and blue eyes. Catalogs usually prefer more of a classic look, which I have. I've worked with Eddie Bauer, Nordstrom, Marshall Field, The May Company, Bullock's and JC Penney. I've also appeared in many fashion sections of magazines such as for *Esquire* and *Playboy*.

Do you travel much?

I've been able to find work in Europe, Australia, New Zealand and Japan. I usually go for a minimum of two to four months at a time. That gives me time to travel around, meet with clients and get work. I also work with agents in most major U.S. cities. Modeling can be a lonely job because I don't usually have friends traveling with me.

How does working in Los Angeles differ from working in New York?

It's much more laid back and body oriented. Modeling beachwear is a big thing. New York is much more professional and upscale, and the clients are bigger.

Do you do any runway work?

There is much more runway work for women than there is for men. The best place to do it is in Europe.

What is your rate?

In the U.S. my rate is $150 an hour, and it can go to $5,000 a day. Editorial work is a different story; you can do covers for men's magazines and get only $125 for the shoot. But having that page in your book means you can get $1,500 to $3,000 a day for catalog work later on.

What do you like most about the job?

The fact that I'm not tied down to a nine-to-five, repetitious job every day. I also like the traveling. I learn a lot when I do, and I meet new people. Every day is a new experience.

What do you like the least?
Not knowing if it's going to be slow. During recessions
advertising is the first thing that's cut. Even if you're working, you may not get paid right away if money is tight.

What is your proudest achievement?
Making it to the point where I can say I model for a living.
I no longer need a nighttime job like waiting tables or bar-
tending to pay the rent.

How long did it take you to get established?
It's come in phases. Some years, I'm "hot" and get a lot
of work; other years, it's leaner. I think the key to getting
work is to keep traveling. Out-of-town models are considered fresh faces and often get the attention of clients.

**What advice would you give to someone who is thinking
about going into modeling?**
Follow your dreams. Do it. Don't let anybody hold you
back. My father was always telling me that I ought to get a
steady job with security, and I would say, "If you want
security, buy a safe." Don't spend a lot of money right
away on pictures. One photo shoot can be expensive, usually a $300 minimum plus the cost of getting prints. And
you have to be realistic about yourself. Find out from the
agencies whether you have what it takes.

LaTanya McKnight, 24,
model with C' La Vie Models,
Los Angeles, California
Years in the business: six

How did you get your start in modeling?
A model scout from Bullock's, a department store, saw me
cheerleading at my high school in Encino, California. I
was kind of shy when I auditioned for them, but they took
me on. I was 17. At first, I worked as a dresser (helping
models get ready backstage), or I just sat in the audience
and watched the professional models work. Then I got to
model junior clothing at in-store shows and do catalog
work.

Within a year I knew how to do all the turns and walks. I got to be a real ham. After one year of college I decided modeling was what I wanted to do forever. My mom did not like the field. I'm the youngest of 13 children, and my family is Indian and Irish. I'm black and slim featured, so I have an unusual look.

A friend gave me a list of agencies; I went to the biggest, Nina Blanchard. She gave me a list of photographers to test with and told me to come back and see her when they were done.

The photographer who helped me get a book together sent some of my pictures to *Ebony* magazine. The next thing I knew, I had a plane ticket to Chicago and an invitation to do print work with them. The result was that I had two tear sheets for my book. (Tear sheets are the actual magazine pages that feature fashion layouts.)

When I came back home, I went to some more agencies and started working with Privilege, which specializes in black models. They told me that Europe or New York was the place for black models, so I went to New York. I was 19 then.

What was working in New York like?
There's a lot of pressure because all the "big" girls are there. I'm a ham in front of a camera, but I found it intimidating to walk into an interview for a job that 20 other girls were going after, too. I did a calendar called "Bronze Beauty," and was selected for the cover.

Then Ellen Tracy needed a showroom model. I begged my agency to send me on it; they were reluctant because I was a little taller and a size smaller than the designer had asked for. For my audition I put on different clothes and came out for a walk in front of the designer and some buyers. I really pushed the smiles because I knew I was supposedly too tall and thin. At the end they said, "We want to hire you. Is $1,800 a week okay?" I didn't even know what to say. So I just said, "Thank you, thank everybody in the room." I worked in the showroom for two months.

What was your next job?
I did tons of shootings so I could develop a strong book. I

stayed in New York a total of 18 months, then went back to L.A. to do some music videos. I did one for Alexander O'Neil, the song "Black Cat" in Janet Jackson's *Rhythm Nation* video. I danced in it—I had won dance trophies as a kid. In Gerald La Vert's video, I'm the lead girl. He sings to me and I sing to him, but of course, I'm lip synching.

Music videos don't pay that well—$500 to $800 for the video, which could take the whole day, as many as 16 hours, to shoot. But they can lead to other jobs in the movies or in commercials.

Is C' La Vie a big agency?

They're a smaller one. I found that the bigger agencies sometimes have so many models they don't promote the newer people. My agency will not hire another black model that looks anything like me, so I get all the business.

What are your measurements?

I'm 5 feet 10 inches and weigh 125. I measure 34 inches, 23 inches and 34 inches—a size 6. I've always been that. Some models don't eat. Others smoke two packs of cigarettes a day and drink tons of coffee because coffee works as a laxative and they want to stay skinny. Some agencies even encourage their models to eat baby foods, salads and juice, but no meats or anything of substance. I have seen a lot of girls starving to the bone. And that's dangerous.

What are auditions like?

I've seen well-known models intimidate the new girls. They'll say, "Let me see your book. Who did you shoot with? Well, I shot with so-and-so," and name a big-name photographer. It can shatter your concentration and your confidence, which you need when you get in front of the camera.

Now I go to auditions with my shades on and don't speak to anyone. When I get in front of the camera, I turn on the energy whether I'm having a good day or not.

What does it take to get ahead?

Good bones and confidence. Some girls go to a lot of parties to make connections, but partying makes you look tired. And you have to be a good judge of character; some girls do a lot of other things to get where they are going.

What do you mean?

If you're asking if there's a casting couch, the answer is "Yes." You see it more in L.A. because the film industry is there, too. A lot of girls do whatever it takes to get the audition.

One of the agencies I used to be with would say, "There's a big party tonight. All the models have to go." I would go, and the party would be in a beautiful high rise, and there would be a lot of wealthy guys. The first time, one of the more experienced models pulled me aside at 2 A.M. and said, "People are starting to couple up and the agency might frown if you don't hook up. But I'm leaving early, so if you want to come with me, do it now." I couldn't figure out what she was talking about. But the way that agency worked, they didn't call the girls who didn't like to party for assignments as much as they did the others.

Do reputable agencies encourage partying?

Some do. It's parties, it's connecting, it's who you sleep with. Agencies can tell you which photographer it would be good to know or if a particular rock star is going to be in town.

Is it important to be at the right place at the right time?

It can be, especially if a lot of other models are going to be there. You have to wear something that shows off your figure. An agency or a photographer might see you there. You need to be visible at big functions. Once you're a big model like Naomi Campbell, that's not the case. But before you make it big, you're more likely to meet people at night than you are in the daytime. When you're trying to make it, you have to be seen.

Why is it so important?

Agencies only hire you to make money. If you're new, you have to be able to say that some known photographer did a test shoot for you. If the agency thinks someone else has an interest in you, they're more interested. The business is a lot of name dropping, and once an agency sees you're in the "in" group, you can get signed and people start calling for you.

Isn't it enough to be beautiful or photogenic?

When you're fresh, it's hard to get signed. You have to do a test shoot with a reputable photographer even if it costs, because if your book is done by an unknown, it's going to be hard, no matter how beautiful you are.

What was the hardest thing you learned as a new model?

Realizing you're a clothes hanger. When I worked at Ellen Tracy, my hair was usually in a ponytail because it was very long. One day I let it down and got yelled at. I was told, "Look, sweetheart, you are only a hanger. You show clothes. Nobody is here to see that you're beautiful; they're here for the clothes." If you let that get to you, you'll really get hurt.

Is there anything tough about modeling once you're working regularly?

For me, it's being married. My husband doesn't like this business, and agencies don't like it when their girls are married or have boyfriends. They even try to interfere. The agency wants to be the one controlling your life, and if your husband or boyfriend wants to go out with you on a particular night, you may not be available to go to a party.

What do you like most about modeling?

It's wonderful when you get to the camera or to the runways to show what you love doing. One of my best stints was runway work in France. Everything was paid for, and I made about $4,000 a week for several months. But it takes a while to get to that point. Any agency will tell you it will take two years to get marketable because they have to get the right pictures, then send them to the right clients. It's a building process.

What advice would you give to someone who is thinking of going into modeling?

You need to be single, devoted to your career, have the energy to be on even when you're tired, and be there when an agency needs you. You're a product. You have to keep your weight down, be clear skinned, smiley and ready to go. You can make an enormous amount of money, but it's a lot of hard work. Recognition comes with longevity. You have to really want it in your heart.

SALES REPRESENTATIVE

**Everyone knows that a salesperson's job
is to help you select the clothes and accessories you'd like to buy. But did you ever wonder
who sells the merchandise in a store to the
store in the first place? That's the job of a
sales representative—usually called sales
rep for short.**

Sales reps (who are also known as sales directors,
manufacturer's representatives, wholesale representatives or manufacturer's agents) spend a lot
of time on the phone. They call up stores to try
to get buyers to take a look at the clothing or
fashion accessories of the designer or firm they represent.
Then, of course, the rep hopes that the store buyer will
place an order.

Major designers and design firms have their own per-
manent showrooms where buyers come to see—and buy—
new collections. New York is "Showroom Central." Buy-

ers go there several times a year for "market week," the period when new collections are presented and sales clinched. Other fashion markets can be found in Dallas, Atlanta, Miami, Los Angeles and Chicago.

Some sales reps work mainly in the showroom; they're often referred to as "showroom reps." Others work out of their own homes, contacting buyers before visiting them at their stores with samples in tow. They're often called "road reps." Depending on how big the region is they've been assigned to cover—for example, all the northeastern states—they might spend a lot of time on the road.

In any sales job, it's essential to have enthusiasm, good verbal skills, a friendly personality and attractive appearance. But for road reps the ability to work independently and "stick with it" is more important than for a retail store salesclerk. That's because customers don't just come to road reps—they have to go out and get a customer's attention.

The job may involve taking potential clients out to lunch or dinner to help set up a favorable working relationship. Sales reps also need to stay on top of what's going on in their particular field, whether they sell shoes or evening gowns. They have to know what the competition is up to and how they can position their goods in a better light. And they have to be able to take rejection: hearing the word "No" comes with the territory.

Some sales reps luck into their jobs right out of high school; others get their foot in the door by taking any job available, such as receptionist, to become familiar with the company and its product. Attending fashion school is always helpful, and some big firms encourage their sales reps to study by paying their tuition. Other manufacturers provide in-house training programs. And, as in so many fields today, a knowledge of computers is increasingly becoming a necessary part of the job, in this case, to keep track of orders and shipments.

Being a sales rep can be exciting, well paying and a good way to step up the management ladder.

What You Need to Know

- ❏ Fashion trends (what stores will want to buy in upcoming seasons)
- ❏ Business trends (what your competition is doing)
- ❏ Computer basics (how to enter and retrieve information)

Necessary Skills

- ❏ The ability to initiate conversations over the phone and in person and deliver an effective sales pitch

Do You Have What It Takes?

- ❏ Personal style (as demonstrated by your wardrobe choices)
- ❏ Ability to take rejection in stride
- ❏ Social graces and good manners
- ❏ Positive attitude that motivates you to keep trying when sales aren't "happening"
- ❏ Ability to work on your own—plan your own schedule, make calls, map out trips and do follow-up
- ❏ Confidence in yourself and what you're selling

Education

Coursework, a certificate or a two-year degree in marketing is helpful.

Licenses required

None

Competition for jobs: competitive
Because the work is demanding, turnover is high, creating continual new job openings.

◆ Getting into the Field

◆ Job Outlook

The Ground Floor

Entry-level job: sales representative

Large manufacturers are more likely to offer formal on-the-job training for beginners but prefer to hire people with at least a two-year degree. Smaller firms are more willing to give anyone with ambition a chance, even if it's a job as receptionist to start.

On-the-Job Responsibilities

Beginners and Experienced Reps

❏ Prepare packages (examples of the merchandise, sketches, photographs, fabric swatches, current seasonal colors, press clips)
❏ Contact buyers and send packages
❏ Set up appointments with buyers
❏ Visit buyers or welcome them to the showroom
❏ Write up orders and follow through on the shipments
❏ Work with stores to promote the line by arranging in-store fashion shows and other special events
❏ Entertain buyers when necessary

When You'll Work

Sales reps who work out of a designer's showroom are extremely busy just before and during market weeks, those four to six times during the year when the seasonal fashion shows are held. Reps who work for major manufacturers have more evenly paced work schedules. In either case, however, it is not a nine-to-five job. Sales reps must arrange their schedules to suit the buyers. And if entertaining customers is part of the job, reps must expect to spend some evenings out.

Time Off

The number of paid vacation days varies from designer to designer and firm to firm, but one thing is certain: Don't expect to take any time off before or during market weeks.

Perks

❏ Use of car or reimbursement for use of own car if traveling is required
❏ Generous meal and entertainment budget
❏ Discounts on your company's merchandise

❏ Designers
❏ Design firms
❏ Manufacturers

◆ **Who's Hiring**

Beginners and experienced road reps: frequent travel

Every rep has a territory, which can cover as many as several states. Count on being on the road frequently to visit clients, follow up on orders or arrange promotional events at retail stores. Showroom reps may do some local travel.

◆ **Places You'll Go**

Designer showrooms are usually very stylish and comfortable in order to impress the buyers and the press who come to see the newest collections. Some reps, however, work from home or spend most of their time on the road.

◆ **Surroundings**

Road reps usually work on an exclusive commission basis. The going commission rate is 6 to 10 percent of gross sales, but it can be as high as 15 percent. Showroom reps often receive a salary plus commissions, which are usually lower than those of road reps because they have the security of a weekly paycheck. Showroom reps who work for New York designers often have a starting salary in the high twenties.

◆ **Dollars and Cents**

Sales reps, particularly showroom reps, can move into management positions, although some companies favor those with a college or even an advanced degree. The first step up is sales supervisor or assistant sales manager. In bigger companies you may move up to become a regional manager. Presidents of manufacturing firms often come from the ranks of sales reps. Another way to move up is to form your own company and represent several different manufacturers.

◆ **Moving Up**

Where the Jobs Are

Although the majority are in New York, the center of the U.S. fashion industry, sales reps also work in the major apparel centers in Los Angeles, Dallas, Atlanta and Chicago—or anywhere a fashion manufacturer is located.

Making Your Decision: What to Consider

The Bad News

❑ Rejection
❑ Hours can include working evenings
❑ Low or no base salary
❑ Little financial security

The Good News

❑ Being your own boss (road reps)
❑ Flexibility of determining your own hours (road reps)
❑ Potential to make big bucks
❑ Wholesale or better discounts on your company's clothing lines

The Male/Female Equation

Men and women are equally likely to be sales reps.

More Information Please

If you call or write the professional association below and say that you are interested in learning more about becoming a sales rep, you will be sent an information package, which includes a complimentary copy of its monthly magazine in which there are classified ads for employment.

Manufacturers' Agents National Association
23016 Mill Creek Road
P.O. Box 3467
Laguna Hills, CA 92654
714-859-4040

WHAT IT'S REALLY LIKE

Brinker Higgins, 32,
sales representative for
Ann Vuille Accessories,
Fairfield, Connecticut
Years in the business: eight

What do you currently do?

I present packages (a cover letter along with color pictures
or photocopies and fabric swatches) of the company's hair
accessories to large department stores. All stores have different attitudes and images, so I put together a different
package of merchandise for each customer. Then I make an
appointment and go to the store. I travel around Connecticut and New Jersey and to our office in New York, where
all the major buyers from the major stores end up. I spend
a lot of time at home on the phone and sending out packages, trying to generate new interest or to remind people
that we are here.

What are your work hours like?

I work about 20 to 30 hours a week—two full days plus a
couple of hours the other days. During market week in New
York, I stay in the city to be where the clients are. You
work until the day is done.

What did you do before?
My first job out of college was as a "go-fer" at Conde Nast, the magazine publisher. I worked at *Mademoiselle* and *Bride's*. Then I met a photographer who wanted me to work for him, and I became his office manager. I left there and started repping for another photographer for three years (sending out examples of a photographer's work to try to get assignments).

Next I worked at a fabric house for four years, selling fabric to designers. I did color forecasting and fabric forecasting (determining what the colors and fabrics for upcoming seasons will be).

Then I got married and had a couple of kids. A friend called one day and said, "Would you like to sell again?" The job was with Ann Vuille, and because it was fabric oriented, it was something I could relate to. And I wanted to make more money. I get a 15 percent commission on whatever I sell. It gives me plenty of time to be a parent, but it also gives me time away from the children.

What was the hardest aspect of the job when you were getting started?
It's hard getting slammed. You always think of yourself as a really nice person, and it's hard when someone doesn't take your time or effort seriously or is rude. They don't have time to talk to you, or they don't return calls or they're late for an appointment. It's you trying to get their money— so their attitude is "You can wait."

What do you like most about your job?
I love the flexibility. I have a job that allows me freedom, pays decently and keeps me current with fashion.

What do you like least?
The rejection. You have to be able to make cold calls (telephoning a buyer you don't know), get out there, drag something around, *be* like Willy Loman in *Death of a Salesman* but not *feel* like Willy Loman. People are going to slam doors and put you down and not show up for meetings that you traveled an hour and a half to get to. Or people are going to meet you and take your ideas and have someone else do them. All that's going to happen; that's the nature of the beast. But you can't let that get to you.

What have your biggest successes been?

Whenever I get a private label going in a major store (making a product for a store to sell exclusively) or get a product distributed in 40 stores, it's a feather in my cap.

What advice would you give someone who is thinking of going into this field?

Sell something you really love, a good product you believe in. If you don't believe, you won't be able to sell it.

Juan Montoya, 26,
sales manager for designer
Lauren Sara, New York, New York
Years in the business: six

What do you currently do?

I oversee distribution, nationwide sales marketing, production and all of the aspects that involve the sales end of Lauren Sara's design company. I call buyers in stores around the country to get the collection exposed, ordered and placed. Buyers come to the showroom to see our collections five times a year. Public relations, fashion shows and special marketing events are also part of my every day work.

What did you do before?

Fashion was nothing I thought I'd be involved in. After college, I was working in public relations and I handled a couple of accounts related to fashion. One account was Nancy Heller (a California designer). I became familiar with her company and was fascinated by it. One day I told her I'd love to get involved, so we met and discussed it. She offered me a job, which I had for four years until the company closed. Then I worked for a sales representative firm that had several lines in the designer market in Los Angeles. I recruited New York designers such as Lauren Sara, Randolph Duke and Patricia Fields to the Los Angeles market. Then I came to New York for Randolph Duke, but that didn't work out. So I was recruited by Lauren Sara.

Did you have any preparation to be a sales rep?

I had no formal sales or fashion training, but I majored in communications at college.

What was the hardest aspect of working the first few years?
Buyers. They're hard to please. Sometimes you may have the most incredible, best product on the market, but to get them to make the purchase is another story.

How long did it take you to get established?
It took three years. I had established my accounts (the stores) and had developed relationships with the buyers. I knew how they worked, and I did trunk shows (fashion shows in the stores) and special events for them.

What do you like most about your job?
People. I love meeting and working with new people. Marketing a product takes so many things—public relations, sales, everything. It's not just sitting there and saying "This is what I have." There are so many ways of promoting it, so many things you can do for a product.

What do you like least?
Cold calling—telephoning somebody you've never talked to in your entire life and trying in a few minutes to get across what you have and get an appointment for them to come and see you. It's tough to get to these people.

What has your proudest achievement been?
The fact that I'm doing what I'm doing at a young age and making the money I make.

What advice would you give someone who is thinking about going into this field?
Do a lot of research before you get out there. It will take time—months and even years—to learn the ropes. You'll probably start as an assistant or even a receptionist. Get in any way you can. I know people who started as assistants at top companies and worked their way up. And know your market and who your competitors are.

Bob Miller, 52,
executive vice president of
the Ann Lawrence Companies,
New York, New York
Years in the business: 30

How did you get into the fashion business?
When I was young and went shopping with my parents, I
liked to pick items out. The same was true when a decora-
tor would come to our home. I seemed to have a natural
gift for knowing what worked with what. Throughout my
childhood and young adult years, however, I was a
performer—I sang, acted and danced.

How did you make the leap into fashion?
I knew Dawn Mello (the former fashion director of
Bergdorf Goodman, now the creative director of Gucci).
She asked me how I spent my time when I was on tour
across the country. I told her I visited stores to see what
they were offering and whether I thought it was appropriate
for the audience. We often had conversations about what I
observed, and she said, "You really should be in the fashion business."

What was your first job in fashion?
I got involved with a designer, Edie Gladstone, and we
sold to stores like Bendel's and Nan Duskin. We created a
wonderful small company and won a Coty award for young
American designers.

Then Ben Shaw, who was backing Geoffrey Beene, Oscar
de la Renta and Donald Brooks, called and asked me to
work with him. We formed a company, Milbo, that brought
designer clothes to the masses. I went into a business called
Concept 7. I had ideas of how I'd like my customer to
look—ideas that I communicated to Ronald Kolodzie, our
designer. Then I had to take the clothes and see that they
were placed in the right store with the right buyer at the
right time. The company was successful for about five
years, but our designer became restless. The fashion business is like the craps table in Vegas. Sometimes you hit
just right; other times you don't.

What did you do next?

I wanted a corporate career. I was engaged to revitalize Kimberly Knits, so I worked as a sales manager. I found out that corporate life was limited because I was expected to do sales and not cross over into other areas.

So you left?

Yes. Dawn Mello had introduced me to Victor Costa, who had a very small business. I was able to take that company and move it to $25 million a year in sales. Victor's gift was making decorated party dresses. We had a boutique at Bergdorf's, so we were in the best shop on Fifth Avenue. Ivana Trump came to buy some dresses for the croupiers in Atlantic City and fell in love with one of our dresses. She gave life to the world of Victor Costa.

What do you currently do?

I joined Ann Lawrence at the beginning of 1992. She had just started a company called Ann Lawrence Today, a designer line of day-to-dinner dressing to retail for less than her more expensive line. The reception to it has been incredible. It will be presented at Saks, Neiman's and Bergdorf's.

We are a great team. We plan what we want the look to be, have samples made and edit them down. It's my job to bring in the parties from various retail operations. To create demand I must make *Women's Wear Daily* and *Town and Country* aware of what we're doing. Then I have to see that our product is sold, made well, and delivered on time.

What do you most like about what you do?

Seeing what you have hoped for become a reality and the next step—having it win acceptance. It's theater. It has become my stage.

What do you like least?

Being late with deliveries and all the excuses for why something didn't happen. I don't like to have fabrics substituted, which you sometimes have to do to make your production schedule. I don't like people who lie or alter the truth to suit their purposes.

What advice would you give someone who was thinking of going into this field?
Decide what you want to design. Doing cocktail clothes is different from designing uniforms. Too many times, people are all over the place, too unfocused and undisciplined.

One has to be willing to do things he or she really may not want to do at first. Who of us wants to go in the shipping department and ship? But when something has to get out, you just do it.

If you find someone who is willing to share his or her knowledge of the business with you, that's great. If you have a sense of purpose, are determined and willing to work long hours, you'll get hired.

WINDOW DISPLAY DESIGNER

Unlike all those jokes about members of the housecleaning profession, this may be the only career whose practitioners happily tell you, "I do windows!" Window display designers play a key role in the fashion world. Their work must literally be eye catching since it introduces the department store or boutique to those who pass by—and, hopefully, pulls them inside to browse and buy.

A sizable part of a designer's time is spent inside the store window itself, setting up the display. But a good part of the job also goes on behind the scenes, in planning the concept, gathering or building the props to be used and, most important, looking for inspiration.

Inspiration can strike any time and any place—walking down the street, reading a magazine, attending the theater,

53

viewing an art exhibit. A good designer always keeps his or her eyes open, looking for a concept that's new, different and dramatic enough to literally stop traffic.

Some window display designers get their start by working in a small store as a salesperson, occasionally pitching in to help with the window display. Others take a more formal route: attending art, fashion or design schools, then getting a job in a major department store that has an in-house display staff. Still others become freelancers, developing their own list of client stores, often through word-of-mouth referrals.

Beginners are usually called trimmers. Their days—and sometimes their nights—are spent hauling lumber, painting backdrops and dressing mannequins. Their work often seems more like physical labor than a creative outlet. But any aspiring designer who comes up with fresh and exciting concepts is sure to rise quickly up the ranks. It's important for trimmers to keep a record of their work, taking photos of windows they've worked on and collecting them in a portfolio.

Designers in big department stores have prop closets and in-store merchandise available for use in their displays. Freelancers must collect their own backdrops, and they often shop flea markets or make arrangements with individual suppliers to rent or borrow a piece of furniture or other property for a credit (a free mention of the supplier's name). For example, the owner of an antique store might let a window designer borrow a vintage silk-covered sofa as a prop for a window display. The antique store's name would be identified somewhere in the setting.

Some window display designers also do a store's interior displays, and then they are called visual display designers. Others concentrate only on the storefront windows. The career is a flexible one that can become whatever an enthusiastic, inventive, ambitious designer wants to make of it.

What You Need to Know

❑ Art basics (color and composition, depth and per-spective)
❑ Graphic design basics (how to use lettering, lines, symbols and other graphic elements)
❑ Current fashion trends (window designs have to re-flect the pulse of what's happening with styles and public taste)

Necessary Skills

❑ Basic carpentry
❑ Painting (you will need to paint panels and objects used in the display)
❑ Lighting techniques (an eye for how light can be used to highlight objects in a display; a knowledge of wiring can be useful)

Do You Have What It Takes?

❑ An eye for fashion (an ability to spot new trends)
❑ Ability to see the finished window in your mind and then make your vision happen
❑ Physical strength (some heavy lifting may be re-quired)

Education

Coursework or an associate degree in design, fashion or art recommended

Licenses Required

None

Competition for jobs: not overly competitive
The need for window designers is growing, as store owners try to make their merchandise more appealing and attention getting than the retailer next door.

The Ground Floor

Entry-level job: trimmer (assistant)

Becoming a trimmer for an established window designer is the standard way to get a foot in the door and gain experience.

On-the-Job Responsibilities

Beginners

❑ Paint or cover backdrop panels
❑ Build or gather props
❑ Dress mannequins
❑ Carry out designer's instructions

Experienced Designers

❑ Develop design concept
❑ Sketch concept
❑ Create blueprint of design if necessary
❑ Supervise trimmers, painters, carpenters and others

When You'll Work

Hours vary widely. Designers who are on staff in a department store keep more regular daytime hours, although evening installations can be required. Freelance designers work at the preference of store owners, so more evening and weekend work may be necessary.

Time Off

Staff designers who work in major stores receive the vacation days and benefits offered to all retail employees. Freelance designers plan their own time off without pay. Most designers do not take vacation between October and January 1 because the holiday season is the busiest time of the year.

Perks

❑ Merchandise discounts at client stores

Who's Hiring

❑ Department stores
❑ Specialty stores
❑ Stores or designers who are in trade shows (some use their regular display designers; others don't)

Beginners or experienced designers: limited travel potential.

Designers usually build a clientele in one area. Even if a store has a number of locations in the U.S. or abroad, each store hires its own window display designers.

The time spent planning a window design can take place in an office, in a department store or in a freelance designer's own home or studio. The actual installation takes place, of course, in the store window, which can be cramped, stuffy and hot, especially in the summer.

Many entry-level designers in department stores start at $200 a week; after three years the salary can double. Established designers start at $1,500 a week. Entry-level freelance designers can start at the hourly minimum wage. Established freelancers usually are paid per assignment, starting at about $500 per window—though that must also cover the cost of props, materials and assistants' fees.

Window display is a prove-yourself career. The ingenuity and inspiration that generate customer traffic can help a trimmer rise within a store or gain a freelancer additional clients.

Where there's a store window, there's potential work. The most elaborate, highest budget window displays are concentrated in major cities, including New York, Los Angeles (especially on Rodeo Drive), Palm Beach (along Worth Avenue), Chicago, San Francisco and Miami.

Although more women are entering the field, men account for about 70 percent of window designers. One reason is that the job can require carpentry skills, which fewer women than men possess, and the lifting of heavy objects.

Making Your Decision: What to Consider

The Bad News

- ❏ Low starting salary
- ❏ Financial instability (freelancers)
- ❏ Working conditions may be uncomfortable
- ❏ Pressure to make each window as good as, if not better than, your last

The Good News

- ❏ Potential for high earnings
- ❏ Being your own boss (freelancers)
- ❏ Creative freedom
- ❏ Having your work get more exposure than most artists get

WHAT IT'S REALLY LIKE

Jennie Hinchcliff, 19,
salesperson and window display designer
for John Callanan Hats and for
Departures from the Past,
San Francisco, California
Years in the business: five

How did you break into window display?
My first job was working part time while I was in high
school as a salesperson at a vintage clothing store called
Tender Buttons in Oregon. Everybody hated doing the windows but me—I thought it could be a lot of fun. So I got to
do the windows the entire four years I was there. I'm a real
collector; my mom and I would always go "junking
around" together. We'd buy things and people would wonder why and we'd say, "Oh we'll do something with it." I
often brought the stuff I'd collected into the store. One
time, I did a travel window using great old suitcases.

I met John Callanan, my current boss, when I visited San
Francisco to check out schools here. I went into his shop
and we got to talking, and he told me to come back in a
year. So when I came back to begin my studies in fashion
design at the Fashion Institute of Design and Merchandising, he hired me.

What do you currently do?

I ask John what he wants—it's good to know what your boss wants. But if someone says "do whatever," then I'll do whatever, which usually means it's going to be weird. When people ask me how I get my ideas, I explain that a lot of the time I try to make a "story" that goes along with them. For example, my first window, which was done in red and black at John's request, had women in blindfolds and hats. The next day John called me and said, "Jennie, what did you do to our window?" I said, "Well, it is black and red!" He replied, "Well, it could work." And it did— it stopped people passing by. John had been used to putting one beautiful hat in the window with a purse and a pair of gloves and just highlighting the hat. My decision to have a lot of action going on was a change for both of us. He's taught me a lot about cleaning things up and making the display neat and concise, and I've taught him that sometimes it takes a little bit more than one hat and a purse.

I'm also a salesperson at Departures from the Past. There are three other people who work in the store, but again, nobody else likes to do the windows except one other girl and me. So we do the windows.

What do you get paid?

I get paid by the hour. It comes with the package—you get me as a salesperson, window dresser and seamstress.

What do you like most about the job?

Just walking around and thinking, "Oh this would be really neat." The best part is when you're in the window and people stop on the street and wonder what you're doing. Then they come into the store and talk to you about it. You meet a lot of interesting people.

What do you like least?

The worst thing is really superficial—it gets hot in the window and there's a lot of dust and cobwebs.

What advice would you give someone who's thinking of going into the field?

Just get a job where you can show your employer your skills. Get your foot in the door, that's all it takes. Doing window displays was such a total surprise for me—it was the last thing I ever thought I'd be called upon to do.

Todd Shearer, 33,
freelance design consultant,
New York, New York
Years in the business: 14

How did you break into window display work?
I was always interested in fashion. One of my first jobs was as a salesperson in a men's clothing store in Hershey, Pennsylvania, while I was in high school. I studied fashion design at Pratt Institute in New York, which gave me a good, broad foundation.

At Pratt I was on a work/study program and worked in the placement office. The visual director of Charles Jourdan shoes called looking for an assistant, and I was lucky enough to land the job. That was 14 years ago, and I still do the windows for Charles Jourdan on Madison Avenue.

What do you currently do?
Eighty percent of my work is windows, but I also do interior displays for stores and showrooms. My clients, many of whom are French, include Christian Dior, Chanel, Louis Feraud, Charles Jourdan, Fratelli Rosetti and Susan Bennis/Warren Edwards shoes. One of my clients is the Kobrand Corporation, which imports and distributes Louis Jadot wines and Taittinger champagne, so I do windows for different hotels and events.

What goes into creating a display?
I deal with small specialty stores rather than big department stores. I approach each window as if it were a canvas and I were the artist. As with any design, whether you're designing a logo or a dress or a window, it's all composition. What I've become known for is working with product. The art work, the creativeness of the window, comes from the product itself rather than relying on props. For instance, this week in Chanel's windows I have the mannequins in leather suits and sunglasses, and behind them on the wall is the big interlocking Chanel "C" logo, done in sunglasses. For a scarf window at Chanel, I had mannequins in skirts that were created out of scarves.

Sometimes I'll have to scout for a fabric to cover panels or a backdrop or a piece of furniture, something that enhances the product, not upstages it. A great deal of time goes into the creation and planning of a window concept.

What was the hardest aspect of working in this field at first?
Making ends meet. While I was going to school and working in the work/study program, I also worked as a waiter and designed displays to pay my bills. I didn't have much of a social life because I was very devoted to getting my career started.

How long did it take you to get established?
It took seven years for things to start clicking. My turning point came when two people I had known from Charles Jourdan left for jobs at Chanel and another store, and then called me to do work for them. Never burn bridges and always do your best, because you never know where those you're working for today will end up tomorrow.

How important is going to design or fashion school?
People in the business come from various backgrounds. I started out in engineering. One of my assistants was computer trained and was a graphic artist. Another one of my assistants was a shoe salesperson for Charles Jourdan boutiques who liked to arrange the shoes and handbags.

All window display people have a wonderful eye for color and composition and have an instinct for what looks right.

What are salaries like?
When I started out, I used to get $25 a night for five to six hours of work. A good assistant can now make anywhere from $15 to $25 an hour. I generally get a flat fee per window, which could be anywhere from $300 to $1,000. I pay my assistants out of my fee.

What do you like most about your work?
The variety. I never have two days that are the same. Every job is unique—the product, the location. There's never a dull moment.

What do you like the least?
Window display work can be physically very tiring. You're tapping your brain for ideas and new images, and then on

top of that you have to do the installation. A workday can be 12 or 15 hours long. And at Christmas, you might as well just forget about sleeping.

What has your proudest achievement been?
My clients are prestigious, and I have the opportunity and the ability to make them happy, to create their face on the street. When you ask most people in New York about certain stores, what they know are the windows. Next to advertising, windows are the most important things stores can spend money on. The window has the ability to either reach out to customers and bring them into the store, or send them scampering down the block.

What advice would you give to someone who is thinking of going into this field?
Be willing to start out at the absolute bottom. Do anything from running errands to picking up pins. Be patient. Put the time in. You have to have a real love for fashion and know it inside out. You have to look at every fashion magazine, read *Women's Wear Daily* faithfully and keep abreast of what's going on. You have to have a love for art and understand composition—and know how to put the two together in a window display.

Simon Doonan, 40,
creative director of Barneys New York
New York, New York
Years in the business: 18

How did you get started?
I always knew I wanted to do something creative, and after studying art and psychology in college, I got a job as a trimmer. I covered panels and painted walls. I got a part-time job as a sales assistant at a men's boutique on Bond Street in London and got involved with doing windows there. My next job was at Aquascutum, which had a very good display reputation. From there I went to other stores—Turnbull & Asser and Tommy Nutter.

How long did it take you to get established?
People started to notice the windows I did at Nutter's. I

started using elements to create surreal or shocking or intriguing windows. One time I rented mannequins and bought Helmut Newton-style lingerie outfits with garter belts and thigh boots and did an S&M playgirl and playboy Christmas window.

When did you come to the United States?
I went to Maxfield's in Los Angeles in the mid-seventies. It was during the punk era in London when everyone was doing shock windows. I started getting recognition for doing over-the-edge windows, like putting women in caskets. When coyotes were coming down from the hills and eating people's pets and children, I did windows on that. It was all very radical and ridiculous, but at the time violence was the aesthetic in fashion.

How long were you at Maxfield's?
Eight years, and it was during that time that I got a lot of other work—film work, set design, theater—because of the windows I was doing. I worked doing set design on "Beverly Hills Cop," "Get Crazy" with Malcolm McDowell and some underground films.

How did you land in New York?
I knew someone who was a friend of Diana Vreeland, and she introduced me to the people at the Metropolitan Museum of Art in New York. I got a job as a display designer for an exhibition there called "Costumes of Royal India." Because of that, *Interview* did a little piece about me, which the people at Barneys New York read. They were just about ready to open their women's shop and needed someone to run the display department, and they offered me the job of creative director.

What do you currently do at Barneys New York?
Most people at the vice presidential level in display don't do design and display work. But I'm still very involved in coming up with concepts and designing the displays. We have 11 branch stores—one as far away as Tokyo—so I'm involved with all of the windows.

Before I start working on a concept, I meet with the buyers and find out what they're thinking and buying. I look at Polaroids of merchandise because it's the starting point for any design. I look at the books of people who have sculpture or painting that they would like to see featured in the window. If we use it, we credit them.

How often do you have to come up with new window ideas?

My staff and I have to generate a lot of ideas; in the New York store alone we have 16 windows that we change every three weeks. The branch store windows change once a month. We send them elaborate instructions about what to do.

Where do you get your inspiration?

I keep my eyes open. I make mental notes of things and take a lot of photographs; I always have my camera with me. In Miami, I saw this crummy old hotel, and the woman who ran it had put glitter on everything—the coffee tables, the lamps. She was a glitter freak. We took the idea and did windows with a room setting that had everything covered in glitter.

Movies can give me ideas, too. I did some windows that were inspired by a William Klein movie that was shot in black and white. And, of course, people recommend things.

What do you look for when you hire staff?

Experience, pragmatism, problem solving. Ideas are a dime a dozen; what I need are creative people who can understand them but who have a production mentality. If I say, "You know those hideous lights they have at the Salvation Army store? You've got $300 to spend. Come back with a great selection." I want the person to organize the trip, account for the money spent, drive over without crashing the van, eyeball a good selection and have some sense of why they picked the ones they did, get the lamps in the van without breaking them and do it all quickly.

What do you pay people starting out?

Salaries start at about $20,000.

What has your proudest achievement been?

That's a hard question because I'm always working so far ahead that I sometimes forget to stop and enjoy a successful window. A window is successful if it gets people into the store or creates a big brou-ha-ha. Window display is like the acting profession; you're only as good as your last performance. It's an achievement if you can sustain a flow of good windows for a period of time. If I can keep my windows hot for the next 50 years, I would feel like I've achieved a lot.

What about your famous Christmas windows?
I think they have accomplished a lot in terms of visibility for the store, and I'm pleased about that. But imagine how horrible it would be if next year were a flop.

Christmas is a difficult time for me. I'm repelled by the iconography of it—snowmen, little trees. I've always tried to find other ways to do it. At Maxfield's, we always did Christmas windows in black. People would ask: "Where's the holly?" and I'd say, "Go to Lord & Taylor if you want holly."

In the seven years I've been at Barneys New York, I've come to realize the power of celebrity. We did Andy Warhol windows when the Museum of Modern Art exhibit of his work opened, and we had an Andy Warhol look-alike in the window. One year, we did Nancy Reagan leaving the White House. We also do live windows. When the Duchess of York was visiting New York, we had different cultural attractions of the city—guys from the House of Extravaganza vogueing, ballerinas from the School of American Ballet, girls jumping rope double Dutch.

One Christmas we picked 11 icons and built a window around each one, everyone from Tammy Bakker to Madonna. Tammy Bakker's Christmas tree was like a giant mascara wand. We showed Jesse Helms as Censure Claus. People loved it so much, you couldn't get near the store. They're already asking, "Who are you going to lampoon next year?" Using celebrities works—it accomplishes our goal at Christmas, which is to bring people to the store.

What do you like most about your job?
The creative aspect, the designing, meeting with new people to put together projects, the interaction with artists and other collaborators like photographers.

What do you like least?
Now that we're a multistore operation, you can spend a whole day reacting to trivial problems. Some days go by, and you think it's insane. You have to avoid getting bogged down in the day-to-day trivia.

What advice would you give someone who is thinking of going into this field?
Don't get locked into thinking you have to study display. Go to school and study graphic design, fine art, fashion—anything like that. You could go off and do life drawing for three years and at least you would then know how to see and to look. While you're in school, try to freelance your services to the local stores. Cover panels and learn to use a glue gun. Get a sense of what the field is all about to see if you really want to do it.

RETAIL SALESPERSON

If you've ever bought one of those "Born to Shop" T-shirts, or if it often seems that you live at the neighborhood mall, perhaps you should consider a job in retail sales. Many stores hire employees on a part-time basis, making it one of the easiest ways to break into the fashion field.

You'll get an inside look at the nuts and bolts of the retail business as you learn about sales quotas, markdowns, shipments and display. You'll work with customers, finding out what brings them into your store and observing what they buy—or don't—and why. And you'll enjoy seeing the latest clothes hot off the pages of the fashion magazines.

If you work as a salesperson and like what you see, then you may want to make retailing your career. Although the higher levels of retailing—buying, merchandising, marketing, executive positions—often require a college degree, a dedicated salesperson can climb up a different ladder.

69

The next step up from sales typically is assistant department manager, overseeing the employees and the merchandise in your current department. From there you can become department manager, training and supervising staff and being responsible for meeting sales goals. The next promotion is store manager, which involves setting those goals, determining budgets, supervising all personnel and developing the store's image. If you work for a chain of stores, you could then move on to area manager. How far you go and how quickly you rise may depend on whether you have education beyond high school.

Taking business, marketing or fashion merchandising courses is advisable. And more and more, it's helpful to have a knowledge of computers since stores use them to keep track of shipments and sales. You'll also want to be aware of what's making fashion news, because customers will turn to you for advice on what to wear. If you're good, you'll develop your own clientele—customers who regularly shop at your store because of your help, and whom you can alert when new merchandise arrives or when sales begin.

In sales the bottom line is this: You have to sell, and the more you sell, the more you're likely to earn and the better your chances for advancement. That's why it helps to work for a store that has merchandise you really like. The clothes won't sell themselves, but your enthusiasm will make it easier for you to!

What You Need to Know

- ❑ Fashion trends (what the important shapes, lengths and colors will be for the next season)
- ❑ Colors (how they work with each other)
- ❑ Fit (what makes a good one; what can be altered and what can't)

Necessary Skills

- ❑ Ability to communicate well with customers and share with your managers what customers tell you

Do You Have What It Takes?

- ❑ A sense of personal style
- ❑ Ability to get on well with all kinds of people
- ❑ The energy to be on your feet all day
- ❑ Punctuality
- ❑ Ability to take direction from managers
- ❑ Enthusiasm for the product you are selling

Education

High school diploma usually required. Coursework in marketing, business or fashion merchandising a plus.

Licenses Required

None

Job openings are expected to grow: much faster than average.

Retailing is a giant industry, and the fashion end alone employs millions of workers and rakes in over $400 billion each year. Retail experts see the industry rebounding after the recession of the early nineties, and they predict jobs in retail fashion sales will remain plentiful throughout the country. Job opportunities for retail salespeople in apparel and accessory stores are expected to grow 37 percent—a total of 433,000 new jobs—between 1990 and 2005. The growth will be somewhat lower—15 percent—in department stores. Many retailers who downsized their middle management ranks are increasing their sales staff because they realize the importance of good customer service. Because there is a high rate of turnover, replacements are always needed.

The Ground Floor

Entry-level job: salesperson (sometimes called a sales associate)

On-the-Job Responsibilities

Beginners

❑ Establish a relationship with customers, contacting them about store sales and new shipments of clothes
❑ Unpack new shipments
❑ Tag clothes with prices and later markdowns
❑ Arrange clothes attractively on racks and in displays
❑ Maintain attractive and orderly look in department
❑ Handle customer purchases, exchanges and refunds at cash register

Experienced Workers (department managers)

❑ Hire and fire personnel
❑ Handle all contact with head offices
❑ Motivate staff to meet department sales quotas
❑ Train and supervise sales staff
❑ Keep track of inventory and reorders from manufacturers

When You'll Work

Work hours can be as long as a store is open. Some stores are open seven days a week, from mid-morning to late evening, including many holidays. Others close their doors on Sundays, most evenings and most holidays. Part-time work—for example, mornings only, or three days a week, or during the summer, or Christmas rush—is quite common. This flexibility is one of the advantages of sales work, because it allows employees to create schedules that fit their needs.

Vacation days vary from store to store and also from employee to employee. Beginners on a part-time schedule will not get the same consideration as long-term, full-time workers when it comes to taking time off. Most stores also restrict vacation time during the peak holiday sales season—from Thanksgiving until the beginning of January.

◆ **Time Off**

❑ Merchandise discounts (within department or store)
❑ Tuition reimbursement for full-time employees, depending on employer
❑ Health benefits and retirement plans for full-time salespeople

◆ **Perks**

❑ Department stores
❑ Specialty chain stores
❑ Discount stores
❑ Local independent stores and boutiques
❑ Mass merchant stores

◆ **Who's Hiring**

Beginners: No travel potential
Department managers: Some domestic travel possible to check out other stores within a retail chain or for corporate training

◆ **Places You'll Go**

The workplace tends to be attractive—most stores make an effort to have a stylish, trendy decor to attract customers.

◆ **Surroundings**

Most salespeople start by earning the minimum wage. Some companies add incentives—a commission, or percentage, on each sale; a percentage above any quotas that may be set; or added merchandise discounts. One chain well known for its emphasis on customer service is also known for rewarding the sales staff that helps maintain this reputation; some of its salespeople earn up to $50,000 a year. Generally, though, salespeople earn much less. Those who rise from sales into management positions can expect a starting salary of less than $20,000 as an assistant department manager.

◆ **Dollars and Cents**

Moving Up

If you have a two- or four-year degree, you will probably be given preference for entering management-training programs. Sometimes, however, if you show dedication to the job, a sense of responsibility and an understanding of the merchandise, you have the potential to rise through the ranks.

Small stores may offer the least amount of opportunity to move up, as most managerial work is usually done by the owner. Large and prestigious department stores increasingly—though not always—require some higher education to enter management-training programs. This could mean they pass over an ambitious salesperson who doesn't have the right degree. If moving up the ladder from sales to management is part of your career plan, be sure to ask during the job interview what further education might be required.

Where the Jobs Are

Jobs in retail fashion sales exist wherever there are fashion stores—all across the country, in big city department stores, small town boutiques and rural shopping malls.

The Male/Female Equation

Sales work is wide open to both sexes. But because of their personal knowledge of fit and fashion (not to mention assisting in dressing rooms) females tend to work in women's fashion departments, males in men's fashion.

Making Your Decision: What to Consider

The Bad News

- Possibility of working nights, weekends, holidays
- Being on your feet all day
- Low salary
- Possible "stall" without college education

The Good News

- Flexible work schedule
- Nice surroundings
- Working with the latest fashions
- Possibility of entering management

You can get the free booklet "Careers in Retailing" by sending a self-addressed, stamped envelope to:

National Retail Federation
Retail Services Division
100 West 31st Street
New York, N.Y. 10001-3401

◆ **More Information Please**

WHAT IT'S REALLY LIKE

Dina Petronio, 29,
area manager of two Warehouse stores,
Paramus and Wayne, New Jersey
Years in the business: 11

How did you break into the field?
I started working part time in sales at a T-shirt shop. I made
custom T-shirts and did some air brushing. Then I became
the manager. I was in art and design school at the time, but
I never graduated. I have no college background in retail.
From the T-shirt shop I went to Canadian's, a retail apparel
store. In two-and-a-half years there I went from salesperson
to the department manager of sportswear, a $2 million de-
partment. I came to Warehouse about six-and-a-half years
ago as an assistant manager/trainee. I became manager and
then area manager within about three years.

Was your career path a typical one?
I worked my way up. Most people start in sales unless they
go to college for four years and come in as management
trainees.

**What were your responsibilities as department
manager?**
Merchandising, sales, meeting the goals of last year. I in-

creased business 33 percent by working very closely with customers and by dealing with buyers, who will send what you need to service the customers. You have to listen to what your staff tells you, too. If they tell you that ten customers asked for purple, that can be very important.

What was the most difficult part about being a manager?

Getting good people to work with you and creating a team atmosphere. That's what gives you stability and consistency, not just within the store but in your relationships with customers. Now we know customers on a first-name basis and have their addresses so that we can contact them. It's a building process.

What do you currently do?

As area manager for two stores, I supervise the store managers. I hire, fire, promote and transfer people. I open new stores and train their managers. I deal with the head office every day, pricing goods. It's very high energy and fast paced. We get in 20 cartons of clothes in one day. We don't have stock boys, so we count it ourselves and ticket it, hang it and merchandise it—which means we get it out on the floor and make it appealing to customers. We don't just have racks of stuff; everything is coordinated. We want to make it understandable to customers so they're not overwhelmed. If they come in looking for dressy suits, they'll find them in one section, and they'll be layered, with blouses right next to them.

I also train the staff. We try to hire people who are in fashion school because they get much more excited about what they're doing. They say, "I learned that in class today," and they can apply what they are learning to a real job situation.

What do you like the most about your work?

Being around fashion, merchandising the goods, seeing customers and the staff excited about the new items. It's a lot of fun, helping customers coordinate outfits and making them happy.

What is the hardest part about being in sales?

Being "on" all the time. You can never have a bad day. The work schedule can be tough, too. Malls are open seven days a week, 12 hours a day, and weekends are the busiest time. We're closed only three days a year—Easter, Christmas and Thanksgiving.

What have your proudest achievements been?

Developing people from sales so they can go into management. I really enjoy taking a young salesperson with a lot of energy and helping him or her develop into a strong store manager. I'm proud, too, when customers come into the store and say, "This place looks great," because it takes a lot of effort to get it that way.

What advice would you give someone who wants to get into this field?

Get your feet wet by working part time while you're in high school, to get a feel for retail. Keep an open mind— different companies run differently. Some have no rules; others have many. Finally, make sure that what you are selling is something you believe in.

Laura Bilotti-LeClair, 28,
store manager, Caren Charles,
Vernon Hills, Illinois
Years in the business: nine

How did you get your start?

I got a lot of my people skills and experience when I started working at age 12 for my father, who owned restaurants and hotels. When I was 15, I waitressed and did a little bit of everything. My father taught me a lot about how to deal with people and be polite to them.

During high school I took dance classes at a college. I was going to further my education in dance but had to quit due to an injury. I then started working in retail part-time in a women's clothing store called Hurrah. I liked my new job, so I devoted my full energy to it. A couple of months later I became assistant manager, and a few months after that, store manager. I was not yet 19.

What was your next job?

After a year, I went to a large department store called Shopko. I was an area manager, which means I was responsible for different departments within the store. It also involved more purchasing, a lot of display work and supervising 30 employees.

I left the job when I got married. Then I did some property management, but my heart was calling me back to retail. I went back to a different division of Hurrah called Peck & Peck and was a store manager for almost a year. Then my husband had to relocate, so I joined Caren Charles. I've been working for them for almost four years, first as co-manager until the store manager job opened up.

How did you rise so quickly?

Because of my willingness to put in the extra effort. It wasn't just a job to me, it was a career, so I was willing to stay the extra time, which is necessary to make it in retailing. I treated it as if it were my own business. That attitude really worked for me. Of course, I really enjoyed sales and fashion. And I asked questions. I wasn't afraid to tell my manager I didn't understand and ask her to explain something again.

What was the hardest aspect of the job at first?

Trying to find the right button to push to motivate each employee. That's a challenge because everyone responds to different things, and I didn't know how to do that at first.

How long did it take you to get established?

It took me two years to make a decent salary. My first job paid $12,000; my second one, $16,000. Now I'm much more concerned with the stability and other benefits a company can offer.

What do you like most about your work?

I love to sell. It's challenging and I like to make people happy. I like to see the difference between when they come in not knowing what they're looking for and when they leave with a wardrobe or at least the start of one. I also enjoy being a fashion consultant. I read a lot of magazines and watch fashion shows on television. I also get a lot of feedback from my managers on what's being purchased and what the trends are going to be for the next year.

What do you like least?

Finding good help, finding people who like to work hard but have fun at the same time.

What has your proudest achievement been?

My high sales. I've made it into our sales club every year that I've been here. That's a nice accomplishment. Earning recognition drives me.

What advice would you give someone who is thinking of going into this field?

Get a selling job in high school, part time or a couple of nights a week. Going to a fashion merchandising school is beneficial but not necessary. If you do, you'll learn things that don't always come up right away on the job, such as things about the buying end.

Investigate companies before you apply, and look into their stability and growth and what they have to offer you a year or two down the road. A good training program is a plus because it will make your job much easier.

If you're in high school, join a club like the Distribution Education Clubs of America, which I belonged to. Ask your teachers or club advisers to get business people to speak. Or interview store owners yourself, which I did in high school. I would call up, introduce myself and say I was doing a project on what it's like to run a store. Somebody on staff would agree to see me if the owner or manager was unavailable.

The more you find out about the reality of retailing, the better.

Ronna Miller, 43,
salesperson, N. Peal,
San Francisco, California
Years in the business: 20

Where did you get your start in retailing?

My parents had a shop when I was growing up in Detroit, so I got early exposure to the fashion business. I also modeled in department stores as a teenager. My first real job

was in New York at Saks Fifth Avenue in the sportswear
department. Sometimes I'd deal with celebrities—Greta
Garbo, Katherine Hepburn, Alan Arkin.

What was your next job?
I left after a year and tried a number of other types of work.
When I returned to Michigan in the mid-seventies, I
worked at a store called Hattie's. It carried Armani's first
collection for women and Karl Lagerfeld's designs for
Chloe, Issey Miyake, Yohji Yamamoto and Gianni Versace
when they were just beginning. It was exciting because I
was the first to see all the European high fashion. Even the
customers wanted to be in my position. I stayed for three
years.

What happened then?
I decided to study architecture, interior design and art history at a California college. I also worked in sales at a San
Francisco store called Yankee Doodle Dandy, which had
antique quilts. Customers like George Lucas and Linda
Ronstadt and people from all over the world came in to buy
them.

What do you do now?
I've been working for the last two-and-a-half years at N.
Peal, the cashmere shop. I show customers the merchandise, put together outfits, keep stock in good order and
write up receipts.

Did you have any formal fashion training?
No, but I picked up a lot from my mother, who bought
clothes for her shop. Even when I was young, she trusted
me to edit her outfits if she were going out in the evening.
I knew her whole wardrobe and would say, "This is too
much," or "This bracelet looks best." I was good with
colors and developed confidence in my fashion tastes at a
young age.

What skills are necessary to be a good salesperson?
First, you have to be confident about your product; it's
easy to promote things that are high quality. Second, you
must honestly want to help customers, that is, make them
feel and look good. If you know how to put styles together
and add unique touches, you can create looks that are
highly individual.

It also helps to make people feel comfortable, like you're on their side. You have to give honest advice about what works for them, not just try to make a sale. It takes a lot of thought to be able to relate to different kinds of people all the time. There's public relations and psychology involved. The more sales experience you get, and the more life experience you have, the better salesperson you'll be.

What do you like most about the job?
I like dealing with the public, meeting all kinds of people. I also enjoy providing input to management about what colors are going to be in next season and other trends I spot.

What advice would you give to someone who is thinking of going into this field?
Get as much sales experience as you can. If you hope to move up the retailing ladder or want to be a buyer, consider going to a fashion merchandising school.

WILL YOU FIT INTO THE FASHION WORLD?

Before you enroll in a program of study or start to search for a job in one of the careers described in this book, it's smart to figure out whether that career is a good fit given your background, skills and personality. There are a number of ways to do that. They include:

❑ Talk to people who work in that field. Find out what they like and don't like about their jobs, what kinds of people their employers hire and what their recommendations are about training.

❑ Use a computer to help you identify career options. Some of the most widely used programs are "Discover," by the American College Testing Service, "SIGI Plus," by the Educational Testing Service, and "Career Options" by Peterson's. Some public libraries make this career software available to library users at low or no cost. The career-counseling or guidance office of your high school or local community college are other possibilities.

❑ Take a vocational interest test. The most common are the Strong-Campbell Interest Inventory and the Kuder Occupational Interest Survey. High schools and colleges usually offer free testing to students and alumni at their guidance and career-planning offices. Many career counselors in private practice or at community job centers can also interpret results.

83

❏ Talk to a career counselor. You can find one by asking friends and colleagues if they know of any good ones. Or contact the career information office of the adult education division of a local college. Its staff and workshop leaders often do one-on-one counseling. The job information services division of major libraries sometimes offer low- or no-cost counseling by appointment. Or check the *Yellow Pages* under the heading "Vocational Guidance."

Before you spend time, energy or money doing any of the above, take one or more of the following five quizzes (one for each career described in the book). The results can help you confirm whether you really are cut out to work in a particular career.

If fashion design interests you, take this quiz:

Read each statement, then choose the number 0, 5 or 10. The rating scale below explains what each number means.

> **0** = Disagree
> **5** = Agree somewhat
> **10** = Strongly agree

____I enjoy working with fabrics and would like to learn more about them

____I have a good sense of color and which ones work well together

____I have enough business sense to know or learn how to figure out the cost of materials and labor

____I know or would like to learn art history

____I know or would like to learn basic anatomy

____I know how to sew by hand and by using a machine

____I have drawn my own patterns or would like to learn

____I can sketch my fashion ideas on paper

____I enjoy dressing stylishly and inventing my own look

____I'm the kind of person who can work with someone despite differences in our personalities

Now add up your score. ____Total points

If your total points were less than 50, you probably do not have sufficient interest or inclination to learn what's required to become a fashion designer. If your total points were between 50 and 75, you may have what it takes to get into fashion design, but be sure to do more investigation by following the suggestions at the beginning of this section. If your total points were above 75, it's highly likely that you are a good candidate to work in the field of fashion design.

If modeling interests you, take this quiz:

Read each statement and answer "True" or "Not True."

____I am tall enough to meet height requirements (5 feet 9 inches to 6 feet 1 inch for females; 6 feet to 6 feet 2 inches for males)

____I am the right age to start a modeling career (teens for females; early twenties for males)

____My clothing size is just right (dress size 6 to 8 for women; jacket size 40R for men)

____I have the right kind of face—good bone structure, wide-set eyes, straight nose

If you have not selected "True" for each of the above, your modeling options may be limited to specialized types of modeling—among them being a fit, body part, large-size or petite model. Now continue with the remaining items in the quiz.

Read each statement, then choose the number 0, 5 or 10. The rating scale below explains what each number means.

> **0** = Disagree
> **5** = Agree somewhat
> **10** = Strongly agree

____I am a responsible person who shows up on time for work or school

____I have a good attitude and do not mind following the directions of others

85

_____Becoming a model is more important to me than any-thing else

_____I'm a good sport and can be gracious in the face of re-jection

_____I'm a cheerful, upbeat kind of person

_____I can stand still without fidgeting for long periods of time

_____I am independent enough to live away from home or spend long periods of time away from home

_____I exercise to keep my body in shape

_____I have the willpower to keep my weight in check

_____I have determination and don't give up easily

Now add up your score.   _____Total points

If your total points were less than 50, you probably do not have the right personality or work habits to function effectively as a model. If your total points were between 50 and 75, your personality and work habits may stand in the way of your finding work and establishing a good reputa-tion. If your total points were above 75, it's highly likely that you have what it takes to function effectively as a model.

If becoming a sales representative interests you, take this quiz:

Read each statement, then choose the number 0, 5 or 10. The rating scale below explains what each number means.

0 = Disagree
5 = Agree somewhat
10 = Strongly agree

_____I like to keep up with fashion trends (by reading maga-zines and visiting stores)

_____I enjoy putting together my wardrobe and dressing in the latest styles

_____I have no fear of using computers and would like to learn more about them

_____I am a friendly person who can easily start conversa-tions with people I don't know or have just met

___I have been successful at getting people to buy things I'm selling or feel I could be

___It doesn't rattle me when people tell me "No"

___I don't have a problem mixing and mingling at parties and other social occasions, even when I don't know everyone there

___I'm a highly motivated person

___I can get very enthusiastic about people and things I believe in

___I am a very organized person and can follow through on plans

Now add up your score.   ___Total points

If your total points were less than 50, you probably do not have the right personality or work habits to function effectively as a sales representative. If your total points were between 50 and 75, your personality and work habits may interfere with your being an effective sales representative. (Some things, of course, can be improved!) If your total points were above 75, it's highly likely that you are well suited to working as a sales rep.

If window display design interests you, take this quiz:

Read each statement, then choose the number 0, 5 or 10. The rating scale below explains what each number means.

0 = Disagree
5 = Agree somewhat
10 = Strongly agree

___I understand or would like to learn art basics

___I understand or would like to learn graphic design basics

___I like to arrange objects to create a mood or setting

___I know basic carpentry or would like to learn it

___I have experience painting (interiors walls, objects, etc.) or feel I could do it

___I understand lighting techniques or would like to learn them

___I have enough physical strength to lift heavy objects

___I have a good eye for fashion—new trends, what's hot

___I can visualize designs in my head and sketch them on paper

___I enjoy going to and buying things at flea markets, garage sales and thrift stores

Now add up your score.   ___Total points

If your total points were less than 50, you probably do not have sufficient interest or inclination to learn what's required to become a window display designer. If your total points were between 50 and 75, you may have what it takes to get into window display design, but be sure to do more investigation by following the suggestions at the beginning of this section. If your total points were above 75, it's highly likely that you are a good candidate to work in the field of window display design.

If retail sales interests you, take this quiz:

Read each statement, then choose the number 0, 5 or 10. The rating scale below explains what each number means.

0 = Disagree

5 = Agree somewhat

10 = Strongly agree

___I like to stay on top of fashion trends

___I have a good sense of colors and which ones work well together

___I can judge when a garment fits and whether or not it can be altered

___I'm a good listener and know how to get my message across

___I can get along with all kinds of people

___I don't have a problem being on my feet all day

___I take pride in my appearance and clothes

___I'm a reliable person who shows up on time

___I can be very enthusiastic about products I'm selling

___I have no problem taking direction and following orders

Now add up your score.   ____Total points

If your total points were less than 50, you probably do not have the right personality or work habits to be a good retail salesperson. If your total points were between 50 and 75, your personality and work habits may interfere with your being an effective salesperson. (Some things, of course, can be improved!) If your total points were above 75, it's highly likely that you are well suited to working as a retail salesperson.

WHERE TO GO FROM HERE – SCHOOL INFORMATION

Fashion or design schools offer courses, credit and noncredit certificates (for completion of about ten courses in a particular subject area) and two-year associate degree programs. Some even offer four-year Bachelor of Fine Arts degrees.

In fashion design, you can simply take courses or get a certificate or degree in what is called fashion design.

If you're interested in becoming a retail salesperson or sales rep, consider courses in marketing, fashion merchandising and buying and business administration. It's possible to earn a certificate in fashion merchandising or marketing; most degrees are given in marketing.

If you're interested in window display design, you can take courses or earn a certificate in display and exhibit design. The degree itself is usually in art and design, fine arts or commercial design, although you can major in display and exhibit design.

For more information about where schools are located and what they offer, check the following publications:

The Fashion Resource Directory (published by Fairchild Publications)
The World of Fashion by Eleanor Lambert (published by R. R. Bowker)

You can get the catalogs of individual schools by writing to them directly.

ABOUT THE
AUTHOR

Kathleen Beckett has worked for the top fashion magazines in the world. She served as a staff writer for *Harper's Bazaar*, *Glamour* and for *Vogue*, where she had her own column, "FYI: Inside Style." She has also been a contributing editor to *Vogue*, *Elle* and *7 Days* and has written about fashion and style for *The New York Times*, *French Vogue*, *Australian Vogue*, the *London Sunday Times* and *Sunday Times Magazine*, *The Washington Post*, *Town & Country*, *Mademoiselle*, *Self*, *Redbook*, *McCall's*, *Working Woman*, *Seventeen*, *Woman's Day*, *Lear's*, *Details*, *In Fashion*, *Countryside* and the former *Connoisseur*, *Savvy* and *New York Woman*. She has written books on travel, entertainment and beauty.